John T. Sullivan

Prayers and Ceremonies of the Mass

Or Moral, Doctrinal and Liturgical Explanations of the Prayers and Ceremonies of

the Mass

John T. Sullivan

Prayers and Ceremonies of the Mass
Or Moral, Doctrinal and Liturgical Explanations of the Prayers and Ceremonies of the Mass

ISBN/EAN: 9783337275099

Printed in Europe, USA, Canada, Australia, Japan

Cover: Foto ©Lupo / pixelio.de

More available books at **www.hansebooks.com**

PRAYERS AND CEREMONIES

OF THE

MASS;

OR,

MORAL, DOCTRINAL, AND LITURGICAL EXPLANATIONS OF THE PRAYERS AND CEREMONIES OF THE MASS.

BY

Very Rev. JOHN T. SULLIVAN, V. G.

DIOCESE OF WHEELING, W. VA.

NEW YORK:
D. & J. SADLIER & CO., 31 BARCLAY STREET:
MONTREAL:
COR. NOTRE DAME AND ST. FRANCIS XAVIER STS.
1870.

Published with the Approbation of the Most Rev. John McCloskey, D. D., Archbishop of New York.

ROME, July 5, 1870.

The Work of Very Rev. John T. Sullivan, entitled, "PRAYERS AND CEREMONIES OF THE MASS," having been submitted to the examination of a Doctor in Theology and approved, is hereby commended to the Catholic public, as well adapted to instruct upon a most important matter.

RICHARD V. WHELAN,
Bishop of Wheeling.

WHEELING, Nov. 10, 1869.

CONTENTS.

	PAGE
INTRODUCTION	7

PRELIMINARY ARTICLES—

ARTICLE I.	SACRIFICE IN GENERAL	13
" II.	EUCHARISTIC SACRIFICE	22
" III.	CEREMONIES	33
" IV.	CHURCH—ALTAR—ORNAMENTS	42
" V.	SACRED VESTMENTS	54

CONSIDERATIONS ON THE PRAYERS AND CEREMONIES OF THE MASS.

PART I.

From the beginning of the Mass to the Offertory.

CHAPTER
I.	FROM THE ARRIVAL OF THE PRIEST AT THE ALTAR TO THE INTROIT	71
II.	INTROIT—GLORIA IN EXCELSIS—COLLECTS—EPISTLE	83
III.	GOSPEL AND CREDO	93

PART II.

From the Offertory to the Pater Noster.

| IV. | OFFERTORY | 105 |
| V. | INCENSING—LAVABO—SECRETA | 120 |

CONTENTS.

Chapter		Page
VI.	Preface and Sanctus	130
VII.	Canon	140
VIII.	Canon (continued)	150
IX.	Words of the Promise	163
X.	Words of the Institution	176
XI.	Proof of Prescription	186
XII.	Prayer, "Hanc igitur"—Consecration—Reflections	201
XIII.	Reflections (continued)—Prayers after the Consecration	212
XIV.	Commemoration of the Faithful Departed	225
XV.	From the "Nobis quoque" to the Pater Noster	242

PART III.

From the Pater Noster to the end of the Mass.

XVI.	Pater Noster	251
XVII.	"Pax Domini" and "Agnus Dei"	260
XVIII.	Priest's Communion	273
XIX.	Communion of the Laity—Dispositions	284
XX.	Effects of a Worthy Communion—Communion under One Kind	299
XXI.	Ablutions—Post-Communion—Blessing—Gospel of St. John	320
Conclusion		331

INTRODUCTION.

HE holy Council of Trent, in the 22d session, on the Sacrifice of Mass, and in the 8th chapter, says: "Although the Mass contains great instruction for the faithful people, nevertheless it has not seemed expedient to the Fathers that it should be everywhere celebrated in the vernacular tongue. Wherefore, the ancient custom of each church, and the rite approved of by the holy Roman Church, the Mother and Mistress of all churches, being in each place retained that the sheep of Christ may not suffer hunger, nor the little ones ask for bread and there be

none to break it unto them, the holy Synod charges pastors who have the care of souls that they frequently during the celebration of the Mass expound by themselves or others some portions of those things which are read at the Mass, and that, amongst the rest, they explain some mystery of this most holy sacrifice, especially on the Lord's Day and Festivals."

In obedience to this requirement of that venerable authority, the author of the little volume now offered to the public undertook, in a series of familiar instructions adapted to the capacity of the most illiterate of his audience, to offer some considerations on the prayers and ceremonies of the Mass.

Apart from the authority of the holy Council of Trent, a very limited experience in the ministry will satisfy the pastor that on this important point the faithful are, not unfrequently, deficient in instruction. A little reflection will also convince those intrusted with the care of souls that many, not of the household of the faith, who assist at our divine offices, would be benefited by a simple explanation of this most solemn and august act of our worship.

To aid Catholics to give the greatest possible glory to God, through this holiest action of our blessed Religion, and to derive from this sacrifice the plenitude of graces which the God of love and mercy intended it to impart, was the writer's primary object. The enlightenment of our Protestant brethren, though only secondary, was likewise contemplated and sincerely desired.

These familiar instructions are now offered to the public, with the hope that what was originally intended for one locality may prove useful to Catholics throughout our country, and to well-disposed Protestants. The writer does not lay claim to originality. The subject hardly admits of it. To the children of the Church, whatever pertains to the sacred mysteries of the holy Altar will always be attractive.

INTRODUCTION.

Fully conscious that "neither he that planteth is any thing, nor he that watereth, but God that giveth the increase" (1 Cor. iii. 7), a blessing from above is humbly, but fervently invoked on the little volume which zeal for the glory of the Hidden God, and for the salvation of souls, places in the hands of the public.

PRELIMINARY ARTICLES.

Before entering upon the consideration of the Mass itself, it seems proper to preface the subject with some remarks on Sacrifice in general; on the Sacrifice of the Mass in particular; on Ceremonies; on the Church, the Altar, etc., and, finally, on the sacred vestments worn by the Priest in offering the Eucharistic Sacrifice.

PRAYERS AND CEREMONIES

ON THE

MASS.

ARTICLE I.

SACRIFICE IN GENERAL.

ACRIFICE, in the most comprehensive acceptation of the term, consists in any act of religion, whether interior or exterior. It is in this general and wide signification of the word that the Sacred Scriptures style the praising the Lord sacrifice: "And let them sacrifice the sacrifice of praise" (Ps. cvi. 22).

In the same sense, the doing of justice is called sacrifice: "Offer up the sacrifice of justice." And so with other acts of virtue and dispositions of the heart: "A sacrifice to God," says the Psalmist, "is an afflicted spirit" (Ps. l. 19).

Sacrifice, in the strict theological import of the term is, "an external oblation of a sensible thing, made to God alone, by a legitimate minister, to acknowledge His supreme dominion, the oblation being accompanied with the destruction or, at least, the change of the thing offered."

Nothing is more clearly established than that sacrifices, more or less expressive of God's supreme dominion, have been at all times offered. We find this to have been the case in the antediluvian age. The Sacred Scriptures, the only history which we have of that most remote period, tell us of the sacrifice of Cain and Abel (Gen. iv. 3, 4, 5). After the Deluge, Noe, on the occasion of his going forth out of the ark, built an altar unto the Lord, and offered holocausts upon the altar (Gen. viii. 20). Then, in the fourteenth chapter and eighteenth verse, we find Melchisedech, in his capacity of priest of the Most High God, offering bread and wine, invoking blessing on Abram, and paying homage to the Most High God. In the beautiful history of Abraham's readiness to sacrifice his son Isaac, all the details—the preparing of the fire; how an angel of the Lord stayed his uplifted arm; how his faith and obedience having been proved, God substituted an irrational creature as a holocaust instead of Isaac—are found in the first eighteen verses of the twenty-second chapter of Genesis. The development of the idea of sacrifice is worthy of notice: 1. The offering of Cain and Abel is of the simplest kind—no liturgy, ritual, priest, or altar is spoken of; 2. In Noe's offering, there is mention of an altar; 3. In Melchisedech's sacrifice, a species of liturgy and ritual is intimated, and the priest is distinctly spoken of, The existence of an altar may be supposed. This sacrifice is remarkable, chiefly, as being the most strikingly typical of the Eucharistic sacrifice.

We also find sacrifices offered by those peoples who had so far lost sight of the one true God as to worship senseless idols. It is, however, after God had chosen one nation by whom his true worship was to be preserved, that we find sacrifices positively prescribed by God himself. A particular tribe—that of Levi—is set apart to minister at the altar. The various kinds of sacrifices are specifically mentioned, viz.: (1) the holocaust, or whole burnt-offering; (2) peace-offering; (3) the sin-offering; and (4) the impetratory-offering. (See Leviticus.) Every thing pertaining to these various kinds of offerings, or sacrifices, is *definitely* prescribed—the victims, the ritual, the liturgy, the altar, the ministers or priests. Every thing in them will strike the reflecting Christian as type and figure of that eternal priesthood and clean oblation for which the Levitical order and Jewish offerings were merely preparatory.

How are we to account for the fact of the existence of sacrifice at all times and among all nations? We must conclude that the Creator implanted in the human breast an undying conviction of the propriety and necessity of sacrifice, or that, in the beginning, a command was given in regard to this matter, and that this command was handed down from father to son—from generation to generation—like the great facts of the fall of the first parents and the promise of a Redeemer. Man, indeed, as long as he retained correct ideas of the relations existing between the creature and the Creator, would not fail to see his duty. The four great duties of the creature forced themselves upon his attention. In the first place, praise and adoration are due to the Creator on account of his infinite perfections. His intelligent creatures, whether angelic or human, were required to pay this homage. The blessed spirits in heaven, around the eternal throne, discharge this duty when they cry out with a loud voice, saying, "Salvation to our God, who sitteth upon the throne, and to the Lamb;" and again when falling down before the throne upon their faces, and adoring, they sing, "Amen. Benediction, and glory, and wisdom, and thanksgiving, honor, and power, and strength to our God, for ever and ever. Amen." (Apoc. vii. 10, 12.) Intelligent creatures on earth discharge the same essential duty, when, in the spirit of adoration, they utter the praises of the all-holy God. But the Lord of lords has seen fit to ordain *how* his creatures should do him homage. Man being complex in his nature, composed of soul and body, spirit and matter, God prescribed a sensible oblation—a sacrifice in which is found much that falls under the senses. Such were the sacrifices which He required of the people of his choice—the Jews. Such also is that adorable oblation, the Eucharistic sacrifice, which, according to prophecy, was to supersede the multiform offerings of the Mosaic Dispensation.

The sacrifice expressive of praise and adoration has been at all times essential. Even before the paradisiacal peace had been destroyed by the fell tempter, and by the fatal disobedience of the first parents of the human family, the rational creature owed this debt to the Supreme Being. Thanksgiving was also an indispensable duty. The stupendous gift of creation in general, and each individual's creation in particular, demanded thanks for the Creator. Besides that first great gift of the Creator, how many others in the natural and supernatural order now loudly call for the sacrifice of thanksgiving! The absolute dependence of the creature on the Creator renders the sacrifice of petition at all times necessary. From Him, as the fountain-head of all good, whether spiritual or temporal, every grace must flow. No argument was necessary to convince man of this truth. He felt it, and, in grateful accents, recognized the voice of his Maker in the voice of his own heart. Prior to the first sad transgression of divine command, the sacrifice of expiation was not one of man's essential duties; for he then stood before his God robed in the lovely and radiant habiliments of innocence and justice. But as soon as guilt succeeded innocence, the duty of expiation, or supplication for mercy, became necessary.

From these reflections it follows, that the present relations existing between the creature and the Creator, call for a sacrifice expressive of praise and adoration, of thanksgiving, of expiation, and of petition. In the Jewish religion, which was provisional and figurative, God himself decreed sacrificial observances corresponding with these various duties. In the Christian religion, He himself, by the great High Priest of Calvary, instituted that grand sacrifice which was to replace forever the provisional and figurative offerings. "From the rising of the sun even to the going down, my name is great among the Gentiles: and in every place there is sacrifice, and there is offered to my name a clean oblation" (Malachias i. 11).

assent, and the anathemas let us heartily indorse.

Canon 1.—"If any one saith, that in the Mass a true and proper sacrifice is not offered to God, or that that to be offered is nothing else but Christ given to be eaten; let him be anathema."

Canon 2.—"If any one saith, that by the words, 'Do this for a commemoration of me,' Christ did not institute the Apostles priests, or did not ordain that they and other priests should offer His body and blood; let him be anathema."

Canon 3.—"If any one saith, that the sacrifice of the Mass is only a sacrifice of praise and thanksgiving; or that it is a bare commemoration of the sacrifice consummated on the Cross; but not a propitiatory sacrifice; or that it profits only him who receives; or that it ought not to be offered for the living and the dead —for sins, pains, satisfaction, and other necessities; let him be anathema."

ARTICLE II.

EUCHARISTIC SACRIFICE.

E now proceed, Christian reader, to the consideration of that "clean oblation" so strikingly prefigured in the sacrifices of the Jewish Dispensation, and so explicitly pre-announced by the holy prophet Malachias (i. 11). The sacrilegious and impious voice of heresy having been raised against the teachings of the Catholic Church on this point, let us place before our eyes the Canons in which she simultaneously defines her faith, and condemns or anathematizes all who pertinaciously deny that faith. To these Canons let us yield our fullest

Canon 4.—" If any one saith, that by the sacrifice of the Mass a blasphemy is cast upon the most holy sacrifice of the Cross; or that it is thereby derogated from; let him be anathema."

In these solemn *definitive* decrees, the Guardian and Expounder of divine revelation, the divinely-commissioned Teacher of all truth, tells us, that in the holy Mass a *true* and *proper* sacrifice is offered. Indeed, in the Mass, which is the unbloody renewal and perpetuation of that first great oblation, Jesus Christ is still the Priest and the Victim. The human priest whom we behold officiating at the Christian altar, though in the fullest sense invested with sacerdotal character, is not the principal in the Eucharistic sacrifice. Jesus is the Priest! All others are simply his vicegerents and mouthpieces. Hence, at the solemn words of the Consecration, the priest does not speak in his own name, but in the name of

Jesus Christ; or our great High Priest speaks by the lips of his vicegerent. Every requirement of a true sacrifice is found in the Mass. So thought the Apostles and their immediate successors. Mention is made of this *true* and *proper* sacrifice by St. Clement of Rome, of the first century; by St. Ignatius, the martyr, who died in the second century; and by St. Justin (A. D. 150), who refers to the Eucharistic Sacrifice as the accomplishment of the prophecy of Malachias relative to the new sacrifice, which was to be universal and acceptable to God. St. Irenæus, who received the crown of martyrdom in the persecution of Severus, A. D. 202, after having related the institution of the Holy Eucharist, adds: "And thus Jesus Christ established the new sacrifice of the New Law which the Church offers to God throughout the world, in accordance with the teaching handed down by the Apostles." Tertullian, who died about the year 216, speaks frequently and in the clearest terms of the celebration of the Eucharist as a sacrifice. He speaks of the Communion as a participation in the sacrifice. St. Hippolytus, in the third century, makes mention of the pure and unbloody sacrifice which is offered in the Church according to the prescription of Jesus Christ. Origen, also of the third century, in his refutation of Celsus, says: "that there are in the Christian Church *altars, priests,* and a SACRIFICE, both commemorative and propitiatory — viz., the Eucharist." St. Cyril, of the fifth century, says: "We offer Jesus Christ immolated for our sins." We find, in fact, the early Fathers and Doctors of the Church so explicit in regard to the Eucharist as a sacrifice, that it is hard to understand how those reformers, who profess to respect the teachers of the faith of the first four centuries *at least*, could have rejected this important doctrine.

Holy Councils of the remotest period of the Church's history testify to the same point of faith. The sacred liturgical books of the primitive Church furnish the most incontestable proof that the Mass was then regarded as a true sacrifice. Those living, abiding monuments of the faith are in the hands not of the Catholic Church only, but also of those Oriental sects which separated from her in the first ages of Christianity. The faith changes not! There is no power left to the Church of Christ to add to or take from revealed truths. Her province is to *guard* that divine truth; to *expound* it to the people; to *hand it down* unchanged from age to age until the consummation of the world.

In the second Canon, the Fathers of the venerable Council of Trent define that our blessed Redeemer, in the twenty-second chapter and nineteenth verse of St. Luke, ordained the Apostles priests, and commanded them and others to offer the sacrifice of his body and blood. The holy Council pronounces *authoritatively* on the meaning of the words: " Do this for a commemoration of me." For the Catholic—the child of the Church—there can no longer be any room for doubt. The divinely appointed Teacher hath spoken! For those who are not of the household of the faith—our Protestant brethren—there are the gravest reasons for serious consideration. Is it safe to give credence to those men who organized sects, protesting against the doctrines and opposing the authority of that Church which Christ commanded to teach all nations?

The third Canon defines that the Mass is a sacrifice, not merely of praise and thanksgiving, but also of *expiation;* not merely commemorative of the sacrifice of the Cross, but substantially the same. This Canon likewise tells for whom this great Eucharistic sacrifice may be offered —"the living and the dead." It declares the ends for which the sacrifice is offered —" for sins, pains, satisfactions, and other necessities."

Canon the fourth declares in the clearest terms, that the sacrifice of the Mass does not, in any way or sense, derogate from that of the Cross. Anathema is here directed against those reformers who pertinaciously assert that the Catholic Church teaches the insufficiency of the great sacrifice of Calvary, and the necessity of a supplementary offering.

To whom is this true and proper sacrifice offered? To God alone! To offer it to creatures would be idolatry. For whom may this adorable sacrifice be offered? "For the living and the dead." First, for the living; for the just, that they may persevere in justice, and even become more and more righteous; for sinners, that they may be converted; and *privately*, or not in the name of the Church, for heretics and schismatics, that they may return to the One Fold, under the One Shepherd. It may, in the same sense and manner, be offered even for infidels, that the God of mercy may deign so to enlighten their understanding and move their hearts, that error will be rejected and truth embraced. Secondly, for the dead; for those who died free from mortal sin, and yet not sufficiently pure to be admitted *immediately* into that abode of bliss where nothing defiled can enter. We do not offer the holy sacrifice for those who have attained the beatific vision—who see God face to face. They need not our prayers. Neither do we offer sacrifice for the damned, for in hell there is no redemption—no mitigation or alleviation of their eternal and inconceivably awful sufferings.

We know the great ends of sacrifice. They were indicated when we treated of the various kinds of sacrifice. They are admirably fulfilled in the great Eucharistic sacrifice. Do we desire to offer a victim of adoration and praise? Ours is infinite—Jesus Christ—the same Incarnate God who offered Himself on the Cross! Do we feel our indebtedness to God? By the Eucharistic sacrifice we have it in our power to make the return of gratitude! Does the galling yoke of sin, and the crushing weight of crime, remind us to appeal to the merciful One on high? What more efficacious appeal can we make than to offer to the Eternal Father his own beloved Son, even as he appeared on Calvary's cross—the victim of propitiation? Does the consciousness of our utter impotency lead us to apply to Him who alone can satisfy all our wants? Let us supplicate through Jesus Christ offered on our altars.

Such, then, being the nature of the Eucharistic sacrifice, such the ends for which it is offered, ought we not to prize it as the richest legacy left us by our loving Redeemer? Let us manifest our appreciation by assisting at the holy altar as frequently as possible, and always with that earnest piety, profound respect, and holy reverence to which so august a mystery is entitled.

ARTICLE III.

CEREMONIES.

THE men who in the sixteenth century abandoned the old and divinely-established Catholic Church, condemned her ceremonial. At this we are not to wonder. A perfect mania for reformation had seized them! If they spared not the divinely-revealed truths, and the equally divine Moral Law, which bore the broad seal of Heaven, much less need we expect them to respect the ceremonial legislation of the Church. It would, however, be a great mistake to imagine that the reformers assailed and condemned our ceremonies merely through

mania! They recognized in them proofs of doctrines, and, especially, evidences of the Unity, Holiness, Catholicity and Apostolicity of that Church against which they had commenced a sacrilegious warfare.

All rational men, even the bitterest foes of that grossly misrepresented and constantly persecuted Church, will, I presume, admit that she rightfully demands the reason of this persistent attack upon her ceremonial.

Upon what grounds, then, are her ceremonies objected to — condemned? Many reasons are assigned; but they may be reduced to three: Ceremonies are *unlawful, useless,* and *ridiculous.* The ceremonies of the Catholic Church are *unlawful!* Before accepting this decision, may we not, with propriety and advantage, ask who constituted the men who make the assertion *judges* of what is *lawful* and what is *unlawful* in the ceremonies of the Church? What weight are we to attach to the judgment or decision of men who, with a presumption and a pride fearful to contemplate, also condemned and rejected Dogmas—points of faith taught by that Church to which the Divine Founder of Christianity said: "I will build my Church upon this rock, and the gates of hell shall not prevail against her" (Matt. xvi. 18); and again: "He that heareth you, heareth me; and he that despiseth you, despiseth me; and he that despiseth me, despiseth him that sent me" (Luke x. 16); and to which He gave the commission: "Going, therefore, teach ye all nations, baptizing them in the name of the Father, and of the Son, and of the Holy Ghost; teaching them to observe all things whatsoever I have commanded you; and, behold, I am with you all days, even to the consummation of the world" (Matt. xxviii. 19, 20).

With these guarantees before our eyes, should not any reasonable man hesitate to accept a decision which charges the Church with having prescribed or tolerated *unlawful* ceremonies? But let us now meet the objection. Why are our ceremonies *unlawful?* Because they are borrowed from Paganism! This reason has been assigned. Where is the proof of the assertion? It is extremely easy to *assert;* not always easy to *prove.* The objection is based, perhaps, on the fact that Paganism had its ceremonies, and that those ceremonies bore some resemblance to ours. Would such fact warrant the inference drawn—that we borrowed ours from them? Must it not strike every honest, sensible man that the Catholic Church followed, to some extent, the example of the Jewish people, who, while they were God's chosen nation, had a grand and most imposing ceremonial, not borrowed from the Gentiles, but given by God Himself. The Church prescribes her ceremonial, not influenced by what Jew or Gentile had done, but of her own authority, and in the exercise of that discretionary power which is her *right* in matters of discipline. She deemed them useful; therefore, she ordained them.

The next objection is, Ceremonies are *useless!* We protest against the competency of the judges who thus arrogate to themselves the right to decide on the utility of our ceremonies. Would they have dared to pronounce the ceremonies prescribed by God Himself for the Jewish religion *useless?* But say the adversaries of ceremonies: Christians are to worship God "*in spirit and in truth.*" Be it so! Let it, then, be proved that ceremonial observances are inimical to or incompatible with worship in spirit and in truth. There is not a ceremony prescribed which is not intended as an aid to that internal worship. They wonderfully facilitate the elevation of the mind and heart to God and heavenly things. The pomp and splendor of ceremonies tend to impress us with a more exalted idea of the majesty of the all-holy God whom we adore. In the use of ceremonies we follow the example of Jesus Christ, who, in performing some of his miracles, employed certain external forms, when one word would have sufficed. (See St. John ix. 6; xx. 22.) In the use of ceremonies we are walking in the footsteps of the illustrious and venerable successors of the Apostles; we are doing precisely what the saintly and learned pastors of the Church did in the first ages of Christianity, at which time, according to these fault-finders, the Catholic Church had not as yet deviated from the teachings of Christ and his Apostles. Ceremonies *useless!* Did the great St. Augustine think so, when, in his disputations with the Pelagians, he adduced the ceremonies of Baptism as a proof of the Catholic faith in that sacrament, and in the mysteries with which it is connected? They were, in his estimation, useful monuments of divine faith. Ceremonies *useless!* Let us hear the testimony of an impartial Protestant witness: "It must be acknowledged," says Müller, "that the Catholic liturgy is incomparable, and that nothing is more desirable than to approach it as nearly as possible. When we enter those vast basilicas at the moment of the celebration of the offices, with that beautiful Gregorian music, which, with the sound of instruments, fills the whole extent of those vast edifices, and see here and there the images of the prophets, and seraphim with their harps and trumpets, that old priest with white locks who intones stanzas from the depth of the sanctuary, those acolytes with their censers, and the pulpit rising toward heaven from the midst of the choristers, we experience really the power of music and the language of religious signs. Separated for a moment from the things of earth, we believe ourselves transported into the midst of a vision of the Apocalypse. This is a public worship worthy of Christianity, and of the gratitude of a refined people who are indebted to it for their civilization." Such is the tribute of an honest mind. The vitiated and malicious mind puts sinister interpretations upon the most harmless and even the most laudable things. We defiantly challenge those who object to our ceremonies to point out a single one that is REALLY *unlawful, useless,* or *ridiculous.*

Enough, perhaps, has been said on this subject to show the Catholic that the various ceremonies prescribed by the Church are eminently worthy of his profound respect, and to satisfy the honest-minded and impartial Protestant that ignorance or malice is the parent of these objections.

May the merciful God, by His potent grace, enable both the children of the Church and those who, in His inscrutable Providence, wander in error, to see and understand our ceremonies, and derive from them the salutary aids which they were designed to impart.

ARTICLE IV.

THE CHURCH—ALTAR—ORNAMENTS.

THE Church, for the Catholic, is indeed "the house of God" (Gen. xxviii. 17); "the gate of heaven" (ibidem); "the house of prayer" (Isaias lvi. 7). Every fervent, well-instructed Catholic is convinced of this, and this conviction leads to that profound and truly edifying respect and reverence which invariably characterizes his deportment when in church. This is the correct idea of the Church. The glory of God and the interests of the faithful demand that it be kept constantly in mind. It will, while exercising a salutary influence over the assembled people, shed a flood of light on many things connected with the material structure called the Church. It explains why Catholics entertain such deep-seated, abiding reverence for their churches; why it is so harrowing to their feelings to witness the desecration of what they know to be holy and consecrated to the Holy God; why, even in the moments of maddening excitement and popular frenzy, when the meeting-houses of the sects are allowed to be used for political, unholy and profane purposes, the Catholic people, by the action of their pastors, leave no effort unmade to maintain the character of their churches, to carry out that correct idea—that the church is "the house of God," "the house of prayer." It explains why Catholics are pained so intensely when they behold non-Catholics, thoughtlessly, it is to be hoped, behaving with almost as little respect in the church as they would at the theatre, or any other place of amusement; why any want of reverence, even in a less degree, in their fellow-Catholics, is regarded as so unbecoming.

A sense of propriety will tell those who do not agree with us in faith, or who do not understand our divine offices, to spare our feelings; and, most of all, through religious sentiment, to refrain from any disrespect in the place consecrated and made holy to God, and at the time in which we are worshiping our common Lord.

It was this most exalted, but not exaggerated idea, that enabled Catholics, in the old world, to Christianize pagan architecture by giving it that wonderful grandeur and that character of immensity which was unknown to the ancients. Even the Pantheon, at Rome, that masterpiece of architecture of the Augustan age, was deemed too low. It was raised much higher. "You wonder at the magnitude of the Pantheon," said Michael Angelo; "you are astonished that the earth can support it; I will place it in the air." His Catholic mind, imbued with correct ideas of the grandeur that becomes the "house of God," conceived the project, and his great genius carried it into execution. The dome of St. Peter's church is precisely of the same dimensions as the Pantheon!

The traveler on visiting the ancient cathedrals of the Catholic Church is "amazed at the sight of the varied ornaments which convert those gigantic masses into a world of artistic wonders. He admires the infinite patience of the chisel which has given life to the whole interior from the mosaic pavement to the aërial arches, and to the exterior from the mossy trunks of a forest of columns to the grotesque ornaments of the roof."

All these are the result of that exalted idea which Catholics entertain of the church—"the terrible place," "the house of prayer," "the house of God."

But whence this correct and most high idea which we have always had of the church, and which applies not only to the stately structure, but even to the lowliest village chapel? From the fact that the church has an *Altar*. "Habemus altare." "We have an altar," says St. Paul (Heb. xiii. 10); and from that article of our faith, that on the altar is realized and fulfilled what made Isaias, eight hundred years before the event, tremble, and inspired him with accents so tender and sublime: "Emmanuel"—"God with us." Yes, we have an altar, and altar supposes sacrifice! We have a Sacrifice—the Eucharistic offering, by means of which we have the adorable Sacrament of Jesus really present as our "Emmanuel"—"God with us." With such an altar, and such a sacrifice, and such a hidden God ever abiding with us, verily, well may we conceive the propriety of exclaiming: "Holiness becometh thy house, O Lord, unto length of days" (Ps. xcii. 5); readily can we understand how and why the Catholic people, though generally, in this country, not possessed of any great wealth, most frequently supporting themselves by the sweat of their brow, are ever willing to contribute generously when it is question of building "the house of God." They know and feel that in the church, near the altar, the regenerating waters of Baptism introduce them into the One Fold under the One Shepherd; that in it the consolation-imparting tribunal of Penance is ever open; that in it benediction is solemnly pronounced on their marriage vows; that in it the stupendous Sacrifice is daily offered, and that in it Jesus truly and really abides, incessantly inviting every Christian soul: "Come to me all you that labor and are heavily burdened" (Matt. xi. 28).

Now, whence that cold, unattractive feature of the conventicles, or meeting-houses, or, if you prefer, churches of our separated brethren? Because they have no Priesthood, no Altar, no Sacrifice, no Emmanuel. They possess not that "central fire which animates and quickens not only the worshipers in the Catholic Church, but the entire Catholic world, and increases, in the midst of human coldness, those harvests of virtues which rejoice earth, and fill the storehouse of heaven."

Since, then, the altar is the great centre of attraction, the sacramental abiding-place of our Emmanuel, "no wonder the religious artist of the Middle Ages devoted himself to the decoration of that altar with a holy enthusiasm! He felt that he was working only a few steps from the tabernacle in which abides that Divine Redeemer who counts the drops of sweat as they fall from his brow, and records in the book of life every stroke of his chisel." No wonder the Church blesses that altar with most solemn benediction! No wonder that all eyes are fixed on the altar.

You may, Christian reader, have noticed that very frequently the Church is so constructed as to have the grand or principal altar toward the East. This custom has existed for centuries, and has its mystic reasons which are eloquently pointed out by Bishop England. He says: "Thus the worshipers prayed with their faces to that quarter where, after the darkness of night, the sun arose in splendor; by which they exhibited the belief and hope which they cherished of a glorious resurrection from the shades of death; thus, too, the Christians of the West turned toward the land of Judea, marked by the footsteps and miracles of the Saviour; toward Bethlehem, where angels chanted the praises of the newborn Emmanuel, to shepherds wrapt in adoration; toward the Jordan, on whose banks the last and greatest of the prophetic train pointed out to astonished multitudes the Lamb who came to take away the sins of the world, whilst the Almighty Father proclaimed his eternal generation, as the mystic dove overshadowed that head yet reeking from the consecrated stream; toward Thabor, where the Son of Man, beaming forth those rays which he emitted before the day-star was created, shed upon the meek son of Amram and the hoary Thesbite, angelic effulgence, whilst the favored Apostles entreated permission to remain upon the sacred spot; toward Jerusalem itself, that city of so many affecting recollections, that scene of nature's convulsions at the Saviour's death, that place of his triumphant resurrection, where the vast foundations of the mighty edifice of our institutions were laid; toward Olivet, whose clouds seem to the lingering pilgrim transparent veils before the gates of heaven; toward that region where tongues of celestial fire gave to the Apostolic band that glowing eloquence which enlightened a world and enkindled in so many hearts the flame of ardent charity. Thus in what would seem to the thoughtless a trifle; in that which the philosophist would affect to despise, or which might be even the subject of his jest for a buffoon, the wise Fathers of the Church, equally intimate with the great truths of religion as with the avenues to the human heart, sought to establish lasting means for deeply imprinting upon the mind the knowledge of important facts, and of exciting the affections to a correct and enlightened, a warm and pure devotion."

The various ornaments used at the altar —more or less costly vases, rich candelabra, rare flowers, natural and artificial, etc.—are employed to add to the pomp and splendor of divine worship. Lights, often in very large numbers, are used even at mid-day, when no necessity or natural reason exists. They are expressive of joy, and emblematic of the light of faith which hath enlightened those who were seated in darkness; or of Jesus, Himself the light of the world (John xii. 46). Every thing pertaining to the use of the altar is minutely regulated by the Church.

It behooves us, then, ever to view the holy edifice of the church in all its sacredness as the house of God. Let the altar especially be for us on earth what the throne of the Lamb is for the angels and just made perfect in heaven—the source whence all blessings, all virtue, every good must come; also the point toward which our heart's purest, intensest love must ever tend, for, indeed, the altar is the throne of the Lamb, veiled, it is true, because it is only in the abodes of bliss that human eye will be prepared and fitted to behold that Lamb "face to face."

ARTICLE V.

SACRED VESTMENTS.

IN this last preliminary article I will treat briefly of those sacred robes or vestments used by the priest of the Catholic Church in offering the adorable Sacrifice.

As a general thing, Catholics know too little of the interesting history of those sacred vestments, and of the salutary mystic signification which the Church has attached to them. Though imperfectly instructed, the children of the Church feel perfectly satisfied that a wisdom worthy of the Spouse of Christ has guided her in making it obligatory on her priests to use at the altar a peculiar form of vestment. The true Catholic repels the idea that there is, in this part of the Church's disciplinary legislation, any thing ridiculous or theatrical. He cannot, for an instant, believe that a divinely-commissioned teacher could be guilty of prescribing, or even tolerating, what would be so unworthy of the Religion of the Incarnate God.

Our Protestant brethren, who occasionally assist at our divine offices, know not what to think of those vestments used at the altar. This is not surprising, for they are, generally, ignorant of the history and signification of that unique form of dress. We do not find fault with them for their want of knowledge on this subject, as it may be inculpable. What we do dislike—what is painfully provoking—what is unjust—is that they should ridicule and condemn a practice the merits or demerits of which they know not. We respectfully demand that they withhold judgment and restrain that propensity to ridicule until they will have acquired the amount of instruction indispensable for the formation of a just judgment.

What, then, is the history of our sacred vestments, and what are the mystical, spiritual significations attached to them by the Church? When our Blessed Redeemer, surrounded by his Apostles, proceeded to the institution of the Sacrament of Love, and of the great Eucharistic Sacrifice, He, in all probability, made use of no peculiar or extraordinary form of vestment. If He did, we have no proof of the fact. The same is true of the Apostles. They wore, most likely, during the oblation of the sacred mysteries, the form of dress then in common use. "It will be perceived," says the illustrious Bishop England, "that however wide the distinction that at present exists between the sacred vesture and the popular dress, the difference was not originally worth observing. That used in the Church by the ministers of religion was, indeed, of a finer texture, of a more splendid tissue, and decorated with becoming ornaments. The incursions of barbarian hordes, the varying fashions of capricious tastes, together with a variety of other circumstances, wrought hundreds of changes through hundreds of years in the garments of worldly guise; whilst amidst this fluctuation of modes, the Church, desirous, as far as may be, in all things, to assimilate the sameness of her customs to the unchangeableness of her doctrines, retained, around her altars, her clergy in their scarcely changed costume." The vestments are, then, to-day substantially the same as those worn by the people generally eighteen hundred years ago.

The Church has, however, attached important, spiritual significations to the different parts of this vesture. To the priest and the attending faithful she made them reminders of the Passion of her Divine Spouse, and emblems expressive of certain moral virtues.

The first vestment which the priest puts on is called the *Amict*. This is a piece of plain linen, which he places on his head, and then lowers on the back part of his neck. As a vestment its use does not date so far back as that of the others. It is the wish of the Church that it remind the priest and the people of the cloth with which the suffering Redeemer was blindfolded. Hence, they should learn to be meek and humble of heart. Whilst putting on this vestment, the priest says: " Place upon my head the helmet of salvation, that I may be enabled to repel all the fiery darts of the wicked one." How much of salutary instruction conveyed by this little prayer! How appropriately is it uttered as we approach the altar, whereon is found sure and unfailing protection!

The second vestment which the priest puts on for the celebration of the Mass is the *Alb*. The word *alb* means *white*, denoting the color of this robe. It is a long linen tunic reaching to the feet, and was a part of the dress worn by the Romans. When adopted as one of the vestments used at the altar, it became richly ornamented, being embroidered in silver and gold. The priest and people are told that the *alb* should remind them of the white garment in which Jesus was sent, despised as a fool, from Herod to Pilate. It should lead all Christians to reflect, that if the worldly-wise of other days, in their self-sufficiency, mocked and derided the Redeemer Himself, the faithful of the present time are not to be surprised to find similarly conceited men now ridiculing His Church and her most solemn observances. This vestment, by its *whiteness*, eloquently admonishes its wearer of the purity of mind and body which should adorn the minister of the Christian altar. Such indeed is the lesson inculcated in the prayer to be said by the priest whilst putting on the *alb:* "Cleanse me, O Lord, and purify my soul with the blood of the Lamb, that it may be fitted for the enjoyment of eternal felicity." Are not the laity, too, by the sight of that *white* garment, forcibly invited to pray for that purity of manners and that innocence of life which alone can render them less unworthy to appear before the hidden God of the Eucharist, and participate profitably in the great Christian Sacrifice?

The *Cincture*, or cord, is the third vestment. It was originally a part of the preceding garment, and served to fasten it about the wearer. Though now separated, its use is still the same. The cincture reminds us of those cords with which Jesus was bound when dragged from tribunal to tribunal by the heartless Jewish rabble. The girding is emblematic of that purity so eminently becoming the Christian people, but particularly the Christian priest preparing to approach the altar. "Gird me, O Lord," says the priest, "with the girdle of purity, and extinguish in my veins all concupiscence, that I may remain chaste and continent."

The *Maniple* is the fourth of the sacred vestments. It appears to have been, at first, nothing more than a handkerchief carried on the arm. In the course of time, it became so highly ornamented that it ceased to be used for the purposes for which it was originally intended. It, too, may well remind the people of some of those bonds with which the meek Lamb of God was bound during his Passion. Viewed even as a handkerchief—its primitive use—does it not invite us to go back, in imagination, to those earlier and more blessed days when a St. Chrysostom and a St. Ephrem wiped away the tears which flowed profusely when, with well-nigh preternatural eloquence, they appealed to the throne of mercy: "Spare, O Lord, spare thy people" (Joel ii. 17), or when, with an unction and a vehemence worthy of the great Apostle St. Paul, they portrayed the loveliness of God's holy Moral Law? Whilst we are thus reminded of their zeal and fervor, does not the contrast between them and ourselves awaken in our hearts sentiments of profound humility? The voice of conscience speaks out boldly and condemns our spiritual tepidity and insensibility. Does not the priest of our day, who announces the same salutary dogmas and the same consoling commandments, feel impelled to emulate even to tears those truly apostolic pastors. Are not the faithful, who, now, with unmoved hearts and tearless eyes hear the most pathetic truths and the most soul-stirring Gospel lessons, invited to walk in the footsteps of their Christian ancestors? The prayer prescribed is: "Grant me, O Lord, so to bear the maniple of weeping and sorrow that, with gladness, I may receive the reward of my labor."

The *Stole* is the fifth of the sacred vestments. The Latin word *stola* means simply a robe. Like the other articles of sacerdotal vesture, it was a part of the dress worn by the Romans. When it fell into desuetude among the people, the Church retained it. Like the maniple, it became richly ornamented. In the sixth century it was decreed that no minister of the altar inferior to the deacon should wear the stole. It is, at present, worn by the priest in offering the holy Sacrifice and in the administration of the sacraments; also by the deacon when performing the duties of his office. The prayer said by the priest, whilst putting on the stole, is replete with instruction: "Restore to me, O Lord, the robe of immortality which was forfeited by the prevarication of our first parents, and, though unworthy to celebrate so august a mystery, grant that I may attain everlasting glory." How admirably opportune this reminder of our fallen state, and that fervent appeal for the recovery of the blessed innocence and immortality which would have been our happy lot had not the heads of the human family involved us along with themselves in sin, together with corporal and spiritual death. The faithful will not fail to see that the priest and people do well to supplicate for innocence and immortality, especially when about to approach the altar on which the price of our innocence, and the pledge of our everlasting life is to be offered in an unbloody Sacrifice.

The *Chasuble* is the last of the sacred vestments with which the priest robes himself for the oblation of the Eucharistic Sacrifice. It, too, was a part of the Roman dress, but has been very considerably modified in shape since its adoption by the Church as one of the priestly robes. It represents to the faithful the seamless garment of the Saviour for which the soldiers cast lots, or the purple which was thrown over His shoulders when He was exhibited in the mockery of royal dignity. The prayer said by the priest whilst putting on the chasuble conveys its useful lessons: "O Lord, thou hast said: my yoke is sweet and my burden light; grant that I may carry, that which thou dost now impose upon my shoulders, in such a manner as to merit thy grace." It reminds the priest and people of the Christian's yoke and burden—the Cross. "And whosoever doth not carry his cross and follow me, cannot be my disciple" (Luke xiv. 27). It also corrects an error. The sinner and the tepid Christian complain that this yoke is galling, and this burden crushing. Christ says: "My yoke is sweet, and my burden light." The votary of worldly pleasure errs. It is another yoke that galls—another burden that weighs him down; it is the yoke imposed by the prince of this world—it is the burden of sin that crushes its wretched slaves.

A few words on the color of the vestments. The faithful cannot fail to have noticed that several different colors are used, viz.: white, red, green, violet and black. By these colors the Church desires to represent the mysteries which she honors, and the festivals which she celebrates. White, says Corsetti, signifies joy and innocence. Hence it is used on feasts of our Lord, of the Blessed Virgin Mary, of Confessors, of Virgins, of holy women, and, in fine, in the Sunday offices from Easter to Ascension. Red, says the same author, is used on the Vigil and Feast of Pentecost, on account of the descent of the Holy Ghost, in the form of fiery tongues, upon the Apostles; on the Feast of the Holy Cross; on those of the Apostles and Evangelists, and of the martyrs who shed their blood in testimony of their faith. Green is emblematic of hope, and is used from the Octave of the Epiphany to Septuagesima Sunday, because, during that time, we are invited to reflect on that blessed hope which the manifestation of the Redeemer to the Gentiles gives all mankind. Violet is used in penitential offices, because it signifies affliction and sorrow. Hence its use during Advent and Lent. Black is made use of in requiem offices, and on Good Friday, because this is the color of mourning.

At the close of this article, may I not ask, with propriety, what is there in these vestments that can be found fault with by any reasonable man? Is not their history, upon which I have only barely touched, replete with interest for the antiquarian? Is not the mystical, spiritual signification attached to the various parts of these vestments worthy of the Spouse of Jesus Christ? Are not the moral lessons inculcated, beneficial to the faithful as often as they assemble around the altar? Why, then, that unreasonable opposition to our vestments? Alas! I fear it is because prejudice, and bigotry, and hostility to every thing *Catholic*, have determined to reject what they think proper to disbelieve; to cavil at what they are not disposed to adopt, and to blaspheme what they do not understand.

May that merciful God who spoke so effectually to a Saul of Tarsus: "Saul, Saul, why persecutest thou me," speak to these deluded and self-deluding opponents of the Church. May they, like the great Apostle, generously exclaim: "Lord, what wilt thou have me do?" Then only will their understandings be illumined, and their hearts be rendered docile to the teachings, and even to the counsels, of that venerable Church—that reliable guide to whom Eternal Truth hath said: "He that heareth you, heareth me" (Luke x. 16).

PART I.

FROM THE BEGINNING OF THE MASS TO THE OFFERTORY.

CHAPTER I.

FROM THE ARRIVAL OF THE PRIEST AT THE ALTAR TO THE "INTROIT."

HAVING in the foregoing preliminary articles conveyed some general information concerning topics intimately connected with the principal subject of this little volume, I now proceed to the considerations on the Prayers and Ceremonies of the Mass.

The subject is one of interest, and, at the same time, so practically important, that I solicit for these pages a considerable attention.

The solemn service of the Mass may be divided into three parts. The first—the Preparation—includes all that portion of the Mass from the arrival of the priest at the foot of the altar to the Offertory. The second—the Oblation and Consecration—comprises those portions between the Offertory and the Pater Noster. The third—the Communion and Thanksgiving—embraces all from the Pater Noster to the end of the Mass. The Celebrant, as the officiating priest is termed, robed in the sacred, time-honored and mystical vestments, attended by his clerk or clerks, advances gravely to the foot of the altar on which he is to sacrifice. Upon his arrival, the first ceremony is the genuflection or bending of the knee. This is done to adore Jesus Christ abiding on the altar, in the tabernacle of His love. He then ascends to the altar, places the chalice thereon, and prepares the Missal. Having returned to the foot of the altar, and again genuflected, he rises and makes the sign of the Cross, saying: "In the name of the Father, and of the Son, and of the Holy Ghost. Amen." This simple ceremony is full of instruction, and is most appropriately employed in the holy Sacrifice. It tells the priest, and people too, that it is the great Sacrifice of the Cross he is about to offer up. "Do this for a commemoration of me" (Luke xxii. 19). It tells him to whose honor and glory it is to be offered. In the name of the Father, and of the Son, and of the Holy Ghost;—to the honor of the Father who delivered up his co-equal, co-eternal, and consubstantial Son;—to the honor of the Son, who suffered and died for our sins, and rose for our justification (Acts iv. 25);—to the honor of the Holy Ghost, who formed, in the Virgin's womb, the sacred flesh of the Victim of our salvation (Luke i. 35). It tells him, in fine, that if ever he stands in need of the aid of God, it is in this function, which demands the purity and fervor of angels. Such being the instruction conveyed by the sign of the Cross, such its appropriateness, we shall not be surprised to find this sign repeated so frequently during the Mass.

Immediately after the sign of the Cross, the priest says aloud the Antiphon: "Introibo ad altare Dei"—"I will go in to the altar of God" (Ps. xlii.); to which those serving, in the name of the entire congregation, answer: "To God who giveth joy to my youth." He then, alternately with the attendants, says the whole of that forty-second psalm which is admirably suited for the preparatory part of the Mass. The psalms are canticles expressive of the various tributes which the creature owes to the Creator. In this psalm, the priest and people unite in praising God. It is, moreover, intended to fill us with joy and confidence as we approach the altar upon which Jesus, the foundation of our hope, is to be immolated. This psalm was composed by the Royal Prophet when, persecuted and in exile, his aching heart was gladdened by the hope of one day returning to the royal city and to its cherished tabernacle. The application is pertinent. We, too, are exiles from our home and true country. We should constantly reanimate ourselves with the hope of reaching it. The altar is that on earth which most resembles heaven, for thereon God truly abides, hidden by the sacramental veils. At the end of the psalm, the priest adds: "Glory be to the Father, and to the Son, and to the Holy Ghost;" to which the clerk responds: "As it was in the beginning, is now, and ever shall be, world without end. Amen." This doxology is very ancient, and is appropriately placed at the beginning of the holy Sacrifice, wherein the glory, power and wisdom of God shine forth so conspicuously. The last words of the doxology were introduced, about the fourth century, against Arius, who denied the divinity of the Son of God, and taught that He had a beginning. You may have noticed that during the Passion time, and in Masses for the dead, this psalm and the doxology are omitted. It is because, on such occasions, the Church excludes from her offices whatever is expressive of joy. After the psalm and the Glory be to the Father, etc., the priest says: "Our help is in the name of the Lord;" to which the clerk responds: "Who made heaven and earth." By these words he admits and professes that the confidence with which he ascends to the altar is not the fruit of his own merit, but that it arises from the help of the Omnipotent God, in whose name he acts, and by whose power he is enabled to perform the most solemn duty of the priest of the New Law. Then follows the Confiteor, a beautiful prayer, which, on a little reflection, will strike us as exceedingly appropriate for the time and place. It is a confession of faults made to God and to all the blessed; and also an invocation of the intercession of those friends of God. It is an expression of humility and contrition. The priest is, as it were, reminded by the Church of that most consoling assurance given by the Royal Prophet: "A contrite and humble heart, O Lord, thou wilt not despise" (Ps. l. 19). Indeed, is not the moment during which we prepare for the great Eucharistic Sacrifice, of all moments, that which most requires humble, contrite confession, and fervent invocation?

When the Confiteor is said by the celebrant, and afterward repeated by the clerk, it behooves the faithful present to enter into the same salutary sentiments. Whilst uttering this prayer, and all others in the Mass, we should be on our guard not to incur the reproach addressed by the prophet Isaias to the hypocritical Jews of his time, and applied by the meek Saviour to the Scribes and Pharisees: "This people honoreth me with their lips, but their heart is far from me" (Matt. xv. 8). After the Confiteor, the priest says, in all earnestness: "May the Almighty God have mercy on you, and, forgiving you your sins, bring you to everlasting life." The attendants answer: "Amen." The efficacy of this prayer depends upon the fervor with which the faithful will have entered into the sentiments of humility and contrition expressed in the Confiteor. Then the priest says another somewhat similar prayer: "May the Almighty and Merciful Lord grant us the indulgence, absolution and remission of our sins." The clerk answers: "Amen." The celebrant and people, seeking the mercy of God, express their most ardent desires as follows: "Thou wilt turn, O Lord, and bring us to life." The server answers: "And thy people shall rejoice in thee." "Show us, O Lord, thy mercy." The server answers: "And grant us thy salvation" (Ps. lxxxiv. 7, 8). During these brief but most earnest ejaculatory prayers, you will notice the priest bowed down in the attitude of the most fervent supplication. Not only the prayers themselves, but the attitude of the celebrant, are deeply impressive, and calculated to awaken and cherish sentiments of piety.

In the prayer said at the foot of the altar, the predominating idea or sentiment is praise. Immediately before going up to the altar, the priest says: "The Lord be with you;" to which the clerk responds: "And with thy spirit." This is the parting salutation which the priest addresses to the assembled faithful at the moment when he ascends to the altar. The last word is an invitation to prayer: "Oremus"—"Let us pray"—says the celebrant with uplifted and outstretched hands. But why this position of the hands? It is expressive of the most fervent prayer. Thus it was that Moses prayed in behalf of his people, whilst they battled with the Amalecites (Exodus xvii. 11). Thus also prayed the royal penitent, David (Ps. cxlii. 6), when, calling upon the Lord, he says: "I stretched forth my hands to thee." And the joining of the hands beautifully expresses the celebrant's desire to collect the hearts of the whole congregation together, to present them on the altar, or his desire that they may all have but one heart and one soul, like the first Christians. As the priest ascends to the altar, he says in a low voice: "We beseech thee, O Lord, remove from us our iniquities, that we may approach to the Holy of Holies with pure hearts." This prayer still breathes that humility which pervades the whole of the preparation made at the foot of the altar. Upon his arrival at the altar, he bows down reverently, and in a low voice says: "We pray thee, O Lord, through the merits of the saints whose relics are here present, and of all thy saints, that thou wouldst deign to forgive me my sins. Amen." The sense of this prayer will be clear, when I inform you that in the early ages of the Church the holy Sacrifice was very frequently offered upon the tombs of the martyrs, or in places which had been sanctified by the effusion of their blood.

The Church, at present, requires that a relic or relics of the saints be inserted in the altar. The priest, as we shall perceive, kisses the altar. This is done through respect for the place whereon Jesus immolates Himself, and also through reverence for the sacred remains of God's honored, sainted friends.

Such, then, are the prayers and ceremonies comprised in this first part of the sacred liturgy. Such are the sentiments which the Church desires the priest and people to enter into—sentiments of praise, adoration and love of God—sentiments of holy fear, profound respect, deep humility, and unwavering confidence in Jesus Christ, the High Priest and immaculate, priceless Victim of our infinite Sacrifice.

CHAPTER II.

INTROIT — GLORIA IN EXCELSIS — COLLECTS — EPISTLE.

OLLOWING the priest attentively, we shall observe that after having ascended to the altar and reverently kissed it, he repairs to the Epistle side. There he reads, in the Missal or Mass-book, the Introit, which consists ordinarily of a verse or two of a psalm and the doxology, or "Glory be to the Father, and to the Son, and to the Holy Ghost. As it was in the beginning, is now, and ever shall be, world without end. Amen." The first words of the Introit are repeated. This prayer

is called the *Introit* because these words are usually sung in solemn Masses whilst the celebrant and his ministers *enter* the sanctuary. Introit signifies, in Latin, *entrance*. The sign of the Cross is again made, because this portion of the Mass, though still preparatory, is more important than even the preparation made at the foot of the altar. The first Christians signed themselves with this blessed and salutary sign at the commencement of almost every action, and frequently during it, when the action was of considerable duration. Thus did they keep before their eyes the great mystery of Calvary, and, no doubt, draw from consideration upon it invaluable graces. In the same spirit the Church wishes the priest and people, during the holy Sacrifice, not to lose sight of the bloody Sacrifice of Calvary's Cross. This is eminently proper, as the Mass is, in reality, the *unbloody* commemoration, renewal and application of the bloody oblation once made outside the walls of Jerusalem. At the "Gloria Patri, et Filio, et Spiritui Sancto"— "Glory be to the Father, and to the Son, and to the Holy Ghost"—we notice the priest bowing to the Cross. This is done to acknowledge that all glory to the Triune God is through the mystery of the Cross. After the Introit, the priest goes to the middle of the altar, and there says, alternately with the clerk, three times Kyrie Eleison, three times Christe Eleison, and again three times Kyrie Eleison. Kyrie Eleison is the Greek of Lord have mercy on us, and Christe Eleison, Christ have mercy on us. The use of the Greek in the Latin Church's liturgy, may express the unity of faith existing between the orthodox Greek Church and the Latin. It is said thrice to God the Father, thrice to God the Son, and thrice to God the Holy Ghost, in order to offer equal honor to the three Persons of the Blessed Trinity The prayer, "Lord have mercy on us," "Christ have mercy on us," is repeated so often to impress on our minds that we cannot too frequently call on God for mercy. We, then, in this repetition, which to the unreflecting seems unmeaning, senseless, imitate the fervid appeals of the blind man of Jericho (Luke xviii. 38, 39), the laudable perseverance of the Chanaan woman (Matt. xv. 22), the edifying humility of the ten lepers (Luke xviii. 12), and, in fine, the holy eagerness of so many whom the Merciful God deigned to hear. At the Kyrie Eleison, then, let fervor, perseverance and humility accompany and vivify our sighs for mercy. After having thus earnestly sued for mercy, the priest ascends, as it were, into the very heavens, and blends his voice with that of the saints and angels, in order to render to God, in union with them, the homage of praise, adoration and thanksgiving. This he does by the "Gloria in excelsis," etc.—"Glory to God in the highest," etc. Let the reader take any of our large prayer-books, and peruse the translation of this hymn. It is a magnificent canticle, commencing with the words chanted by the heavenly host, in the hearing of the humble shepherds of Bethlehem, on that ever-blessed night in which Jesus, the promised Messiah, was born. "Glory to God in the highest, and on earth peace to men of good-will" (Luke ii.). If the birth of Christ gave glory to God, and brought peace to fallen man, that glory and that peace were consummated only on the Cross, and the mysteries of Calvary are represented and really perpetuated in the Adorable Sacrifice of our altar. Hence the propriety of this canticle in the Mass. It is to be noticed that, at certain words of this hymn, the priest bows his head in reverence. This takes place, chiefly, at the words expressive of the four great ends of the Sacrifice; first, praise and adoration: "Adoramus te"—"We adore thee;" secondly, thanksgiving: "Gratias agimus tibi"—"We thank thee;" thirdly and fourthly, petition, grace and pardon: "Suscipe deprecationem nostram"—"Receive our prayer." At the conclusion of the "Gloria in excelsis," the priest again signs himself with the sign of the Cross, to signify that the most excellent prayer avails not except through Jesus Christ crucified. Immediately after the "Gloria in excelsis," the priest kisses the altar, and, having turned to the assembled people, says: "Dominus vobiscum"—"The Lord be with you." He kisses the altar, which is a figure of Jesus Christ, to express his filial affection toward the Saviour, and to receive from Him the salutation of peace, in order that, as the vicegerent of Christ, he may impart it to the faithful. Instead of the

"Dominus vobiscum," a bishop says: "Pax vobis"—"Peace be with you"—because, by his exalted position, he more strikingly represents Jesus Christ, who frequently saluted his Apostles with the words: "Peace be with you" (John xx. 21, 26). The priest goes to the Epistle corner and says aloud: "Oremus"—"Let us pray." The faithful are all invited to unite in this prayer. Let them profit by the invitation and pour forth their hearts in strains of fervent, humble supplication. The prayer or prayers here said are termed, in the language of the Church, "Collects," either because they are said for the faithful *collected* together, or because the intentions of the whole congregation are, as it were, collected together and prayed for, or, again, because it is a summary of what is asked of God. At the name of Jesus, the priest again bows to the Cross, acknowledging that it is only through

Christ *crucified* that he and the people can pray becomingly and profitably. For the same reason, the prayers always terminate in the following or equivalent words: "Per Dominum nostrum Jesum Christum," etc.—"Through Jesus Christ our Lord," etc. The "Amen" said by the server, in the name of the congregation, is the expression of assent to what has been prayed for, and of great desire that it may be obtained.

After the Collects, or Prayers, follows the Epistle. For the proper understanding of this and what succeeds, it is to be remarked that this first or preparatory part of the Mass was formerly called the Mass of the Catechumens, that is, of those preparing for holy Baptism. They needed instruction, and this was imparted to them in the Epistle, Gospel, and in the explanations made on the portions of Sacred Writ read to them on those occasions. In the Collects we begged to know God's holy will. Now, the sacred Scriptures and the Epistle and Gospel make known to us that holy will. The Epistle, or Lesson, which is first read, is always either some part of the Old Testament, or of the Acts of the Apostles, or of their Epistles. This order is observed because the Old Testament was a preparation for the New; or because Jesus Christ sent his disciples before Himself (Luke x. 1). The Church has at all times been very solicitous concerning the proper instruction of the adults whom she intended to admit to the laver of regeneration. She wishes them to be thoroughly grounded in the faith, that they may not, like the votaries of error around her, be "tossed to and fro and carried about by every wind of doctrine" (Eph. iv. 14). After the Epistle, the server says: "Deo gratias" —"Thanks be to God." How proper it is to return thanks for the instruction conveyed to us in God's saving Word! The "Gradual," or Tract, consists of the few words that follow the Epistle. Alleluia is a Hebrew word expressing praise to God, and not simple praise only, but praise accompanied with the plenitude of joy and exultation.

Even at this early stage of our considerations and explanations of the prayers and ceremonies of the Mass, are we not convinced that a superhuman wisdom has guided the holy Church in the choice of the prayers and in the selection of the rites and ceremonies? If so, do we not feel that our interests and the respect and obedience due to a divinely-guided Church, demand that we should reverently and devoutly endeavor to profit by those things which have been ordained for our edification and instruction? God grant that those who read these familiar explanations may more and more faithfully correspond with the designs of His holy Church.

CHAPTER III.

GOSPEL AND CREED.

AT the end of the Epistle and Gradual, the faithful assisting at the holy Sacrifice notice that the priest repairs to the middle of the altar; that he remains there for a few moments bowed down in the attitude of fervent prayer; that he then goes to the Gospel side. During these moments of prayer, the clerk removes the Missal or Mass-book to the right-hand side of the crucifix. The mystical signification of the removal of the Missal is worthy of notice. It has already been said that

the portions of the sacred Scriptures read in the Epistle were frequently taken from the Old Testament. With this fact borne in mind, the mystical signification attached to the removal of the book to the Gospel side is readily perceived and appreciated. It represents the "translation of the law and authority from the Aaronitic to the Apostolic priesthood." It signifies that the saving truths of divine revelation, which the Jews rejected, have been announced to the Gentiles.

We saw the officiating priest go to the middle of the altar. He is reverently bowed down! The most casual observer cannot fail to conclude that he is engaged in fervent prayer. But what is the prayer which at this moment absorbs his whole attention? "O Almighty, who didst purify the lips of Isaias the prophet with a burning coal, cleanse my heart and lips; and vouchsafe, of thy gracious mercy, so to purify me, that I may be able worthily to announce thy holy Gospel." Here, then, we behold the minister of the Catholic Church, not content with the preparation made at the foot of the altar, nor with those prayers uttered after his ascent, appealing in a special manner to the Omnipotent God to render him worthy to utter those divine words. This is done every day, in the holy Sacrifice, at the thousands of altars upon which the pure oblation is made, from the rising of the sun to the going down thereof! How, then, could those who are not of our holy faith charge us with want of respect for the sacred Scriptures? Must not the grossest ignorance or the most culpable malice have led to the glaringly unjust misrepresentation? On this subject Bishop England says: "The affection of the faithful and their veneration for the sacred Scriptures have always been exceedingly great; and the conduct of the Church, arising from these sentiments, has been greatly misunderstood by several who do not examine. At the present day, the Spouse of Christ regards the sacred Volume as one of the most precious deposits entrusted to her guardianship. She feels it to be her duty to preserve the context pure, entire and unaltered—not only to preserve the words, but to testify to their meaning—in discharge of the high commission of the Saviour. This is done, not by novel, arbitrary interpretations, but by declaring what was always the sense in which the passages of Holy Writ were understood by the Christian world. Hence she forbids her children to receive or to use any copies which have not been examined by competent authority; and thus, through the lapse of ages and the convulsions of human institutions, notwithstanding the efforts of her adversaries, she has kept these venerable pages free from human corruptions. She requires also of her children that they shall conform their minds to that meaning which was received in the beginning, with the books themselves, from the inspired compilers, and that they shall never interpret them otherwise than according to the unanimous consent of the Fathers who, in every age, have given to us the uninterrupted testimony of this original signification. She knows of no principle of common sense or of religion, upon which any individual could, after the lapse of centuries, assume to himself the prerogative of discovering the true meaning of any passage of the Bible to be different from that which is thus testified by the unanimous declaration of the great bulk of Christendom. For this would, in fact, be a new revelation. If the vast majority has been unanimous, and yet involved in error, upon what principle will a divided and discordant minority claim to be correct? If there be no plain and certain mode of knowing the meaning of the passages of the Word of God, of what value is their possession? She cannot consent to put the great book of divine revelation upon a par with the riddles and enigmas of heathen oracles. In her assemblies, she proclaims the sacred writings in a dead and unchanging language, in which during centuries they have been preserved, but she allows exact translations in the vernacular tongue; she requires that they be frequently collated with the standard, and that they be explained by her commissioned expositors. Her pastors are not permitted to introduce opinions of their own, but they are bound before many witnesses to declare openly what had been openly placed in their keeping. The Persian, the Chinese, the

Italian, the German, the American and the Spaniard must agree, in doctrine, with the Numidian and the Moor, because the revelation of a God of truth must every where be consistent with itself. She calls the license to introduce new and discordant interpretations a sanction to disseminate error, and the propagation of error she looks upon as the worst abuse of liberty."

The priest having by humble, fervent prayer prepared himself to read the Gospel, goes to the book, and then says in a loud voice: "Dominus vobiscum"—"The Lord be with you." Immediately afterward he tells the assembled faithful from which Evangelist he intends to read. This he does by the words: "Initium, or sequentia, sancti Evangelii secundum N."—"The beginning, or the sequence of the holy Gospel according to N." Here he mentions the name of the Evangelist. Whilst saying these words, the priest signs himself with the sign of the Cross, upon his forehead, his lips, and his breast; on the forehead, to denote that, through the merits of the Cross, he will never be ashamed of the truth conveyed by the holy Gospel; on his lips, to indicate that he is ever ready fearlessly to profess his faith; and on his breast, to show that his heart cherishes what he is not ashamed to admit, or afraid to proclaim. The clerk responds: "Gloria tibi Domine"—"Glory be to thee, O Lord." Glory to thee, O Lord, for having dispelled the mists of our ignorance by the light of truth, for consoling us in our sorrows by the unction of thy blessed Word, and for strengthening our weakness by the help of thy saving precepts. At the end of the reading of the Gospel, the clerk responds, praising the Lord for his holy revelation: "Laus tibi Christe"— "Praise be to thee, O Christ." The priest then kisses the Gospel through respect for the sacred Word, and says: ' May our sins be blotted out through the holy Gospel."

We have seen that the first part of the Mass—the Mass of the Catechumens, or the Preparation—ended with the Credo. The Creed is a compendium of the principal dogmas which the Church requires us to believe. It is said or sung after the Instruction, or sermon. Notice how appropriately this confession of faith is placed in this particular part of the liturgy. It expresses our assent to the truths announced in the Epistle, Gospel, and the fuller details contained in the sermon itself. There are several creeds or confessions of faith, all, of course, expressing the same faith—"One faith" (Eph. iv. 5). In what, then, do they differ? In the fact that some are more detailed, more explicit in the declaration of that "one faith." But why that greater explicitness? Because the Church, without making any change in the faith, has added such expressions and explanations as were required to confound the various heresiarchs who have, from the beginning, assailed the faith. There are five principal creeds. The Apostles' Creed, coming down from the days of the Apostles; the Nicene Creed, drawn up in the General Council of Nice, in the year 325, against Arius and his followers, who denied the divinity of Jesus Christ; the Creed of Constantinople, so called because made or drawn up in that city by the General Council held there in the year 381. This creed differs but little from the foregoing. The divinity of the Holy Ghost, which was maintained in that council against Macedonius, is more explicitly professed. The fourth is the Athanasian Creed, so called because that illustrious champion of the faith is said, though probably incorrectly, to be the author of this formulary; and fifthly, the

Creed of Pius IV., which bishops, doctors and converts are required explicitly to profess. During the Creed, at the words: "Et incarnatus est de Spiritu Sancto ex Maria Virgine et homo factus est"—"And was incarnated by the Holy Ghost of the Virgin Mary, and He was made man," the priest and people bend the knee, in honor of the great mystery of the Incarnation.

In concluding this third chapter, let us resolve to enter most seriously into the designs of the Church, our holy Mother. She wishes each ceremony to contribute to our edification and instruction. Let us with the eye of faith see the wisdom which is evinced even in the minutest of her ceremonial prescriptions. To the announcements of the Gospel let us bring all that respect to which the Word of God is entitled, and to its salutary precepts, all that docility without which they will prove, not means of salvation, but occasions of greater culpability, and perhaps of damnation. To the profession of faith made in the Creed during the holy Sacrifice, we should always give our fullest assent, and what we profess with our lips we should, in all places and at all times, confirm by our conduct. Thus only shall we give glory to the God of our altar, and draw down on ourselves the graces and blessings which He is ever ready to bestow on those assembled to offer to His honor the great Eucharistic Sacrifice.

PART II.

FROM THE OFFERTORY TO THE PATER NOSTER.

CHAPTER IV.

OFFERTORY — ITS PRAYERS AND CEREMONIES.

THE second part of the Mass—the Oblation and Consecration — comprises all those portions of the sacred liturgy between the Offertory and the Pater Noster. The Gospel, with the homily or familiar instruction given upon it, was

the end of the Mass of the Catechumens. The Creed, of which we have already treated, was in all probability not said before those who had not been baptized and initiated in the mysteries of the faith. It even appears almost certain that the introduction of this profession or confession of faith into the liturgy does not date any farther back than the fifth or sixth century. The "Dominus vobiscum"—"The Lord be with you"— is said after the Creed, or after the Gospel when the Creed is not said. In this instance these words may be regarded as a parting salutation addressed to the Catechumens who were sent away at this point of the Mass, or they may have been uttered in the sense of an invocation of special blessing in behalf of those who were so happy and so privileged as to remain at the most solemn and august mystery of the Eucharistic Sacrifice. After the "Dominus vobiscum," the priest, turning to the altar, says aloud: "Oremus"—"Let us pray." He prays *aloud* in order to invite the people to renew their fervor in prayer—to unite their petitions with his; in a word, by the union of prayer, to participate in the graces and blessings of this most solemn part of the Mass. The prayer which he then says is a verse of the holy Scriptures. In solemn Masses it was sung whilst the celebrant made the oblation or offering. Hence its name, Offertory. This part itself of the Mass is called Offertory, because it is here, as you will notice, that the bread and wine are *offered* for the Sacrifice. Oblation is essential to every sacrifice. In the early ages of the Church, the faithful made at this point of the liturgy their offering, not only of what was required for the Sacrifice, but of whatever was necessary for the support of their pastors, and for the wants of the poor and the sick.

Out of the general offerings, an officer of the altar—the deacon—selected what was needed for the altar, for the Sacrifice. This custom gradually disappeared. The fact that the ministers of the Church found it necessary to use, in the Sacrifice, a bread and wine more carefully prepared than those presented by the faithful, led probably to its discontinuance. The collection taken up after the Gospel at present may be considered a vestige of this ancient custom. The offering made by the priest is bread and wine. Why bread and wine? Because the Sacrifice which he is about to offer is the same that Jesus Christ Himself offered (Matt. xxvi. 26, 27, 28; Mark xiv. 22, 23, 24; Luke xxii. 17, 18, 19, 20; 1 Cor. xi. 24, 25). This bread must be wheaten, and the wine must be the juice of the grape. The Latin Church prescribes the use of *unleavened* bread. Hence a priest of the Church cannot, without grievous sin, make use of any other. However, it is well understood that this command of the Church is only *disciplinary*. The validity of the Sacrifice, or the substance of the Sacrament, is not interfered with when *leavened* bread is used.

Just before the Oblation, the priest spreads out the *Corporal*, or linen cloth upon which the sacred body of Jesus is to repose. Then he takes the Patena, or little plate containing the bread, and in a low voice he says: "Accept, O Holy Father, Almighty and Eternal God, this unspotted Host, which I, thy unworthy servant, offer unto thee, my living and true God, for my innumerable sins, offences and negligences, and for all here present, as also for all faithful Christians both living and dead, that it may avail both me and them unto life everlasting. Amen." Before laying the bread just offered upon the Corporal, he makes the sign of the Cross, mindful that it is the Sacrifice of the Cross he is about to renew. We are invited to ponder attentively the many useful instructions conveyed by this important prayer. To whom is the oblation made? To the Holy Father, Almighty and Eternal God. To none else! Not to Mary, the highest and most honored of God's creatures; not to angels or archangels; not to patriarch, or prophet, or saint. To God alone may sacrifice be offered. How futile, then, and malevolent are the charges made against the Church, that she offers sacrifice to the Blessed Virgin and the saints! By whom is the offering made? Though the priest says: "Which I, thy unworthy servant, offer," etc., still the Catholic knows well that Jesus Christ is the principal offerer. He is our High Priest, as St. Paul teaches (Heb. v. 10). Even as He is "always living to make intercession for us" (Heb. vii. 25) in heaven, before the throne of His Father, so His duly-appointed agents make oblations in His name, and renew that one great Sacrifice which superseded the manifold sacrifices of an imperfect dispensation. The Catholic Church is also an offerer, for, mystically, she is that body of which Jesus is the head. Then the priest is an offerer, and rightfully does he say: "Receive, Holy Father, Almighty and Eternal God, this spotless Host, which I, thy unworthy servant, offer to thee," etc., for he has been chosen and anointed to minister at the altar, and empowered in his ordination to act as the agent, and speak as the mouthpiece of the great High Priest, Christ Jesus. In fine, the faithful are offerers in this oblation, not in the *strict sense* of the word, but only as uniting in spirit with the priest, who, in the strictest and fullest sense, alone is the immediate and properly so-called offerer and minister of the Eucharistic

Sacrifice. What motives of fervor presented to the priest and to those assembled around the altar! What inducements to bring to the discharge of this solemn function of oblation that purity of soul, that perfection of attention, and that aggregate of holy dispositions becoming so sacred an action! What is the offering made? At this point of the Sacrifice, merely bread and wine—material elements; but, in a few moments, by the omnipotent word of God, to be changed *truly, really* and *substantially* into the body and blood of the spotless Victim once offered on Calvary's Cross. Do the worldly wise hesitate to believe the promised transubstantiation? Are they embarrassed at the difficulty of such a change of substances? They certainly do not question God's power to effect the change! The Psalmist tells us: "He spoke and they were created, He commanded and they were made" (Ps. cxl.

5). Do they question God's right to delegate that power to creatures? Who dares place limits to Omnipotence? Do they question the *fact* that this power has been delegated? What, then, do they understand by the words of St. Luke (xxii. 19).: "And taking bread, he (Jesus) gave thanks, and brake, and gave to them, saying: This is my body which is given for you: *Do this for a commemoration of me.*" Ah! worldly-wise, ye *reformers of God's* work, learn of the great Apostle to the Romans (Romans xii. 3) "not to be more wise than it behooveth to be wise; but to be wise unto sobriety." The *Catholic Church*, with which Jesus Himself promised to abide to the end of time (Matt. xxviii. 20); whose province is to *teach* (Matt. xxviii. 19), and to which the ever-abiding Paraclete, or Holy Ghost, was sent as the Teacher of all truth (John xiv. 26), tells us that Jesus Christ effected the change in question, and delegated to his pastors the power to do the same. What the Church teaches to-day has been her teaching since the days of the Apostles. *You*, self-reliant, worldly-wise, deny the fact! Were not the point at issue of too serious a nature, of too vast an importance, your presumption would, in truth, be as amusing as the silly thoughts of a child.

Let us resume our moral reflections on this part of the Mass. It behooves us to learn from the fact that Jesus Christ is the High Priest who makes the oblation; that the entire Catholic Church participates in the offering; that it is an oblation for the living and the dead; that the glory of God and the highest interests of man are promoted by it, how important, how awfully solemn, is this part of the sacred liturgy, how superlatively cogent are the reasons demanding on our part the most perfect dispositions!

After the offering of the bread and wine, the priest goes to the Epistle side of the altar, where he finds the clerk having the wine and water. The priest first pours wine into the chalice, and then, having blessed the water with the sign of the Cross, mixes a small quantity with the wine, saying: "O God, who, in creating human nature, hast wonderfully dignified and still more wonderfully reformed it, grant that by the mystery of this water and wine, we may be made partakers of His divine nature who vouchsafed to become partaker of our human nature, Jesus Christ our Lord, thy Son, who with thee, in the unity of the Holy Ghost, liveth and reigneth, world without end. Amen." The mixture of the water with the wine has a mystical, spiritual signification. It forcibly reminds us of that memorable circumstance related by the beloved disciple St. John (xix. 34): "But one of the soldiers with a spear opened his side, and immediately there came out blood and water." Besides, tradition informs us that in the changing of the bread and wine into His body and blood, Jesus mixed water with the wine. Liturgists tell us that the wine represents the divine nature, and the water, the human. By the mixture of the two material elements, the union of the two natures— the divine and the human—in the one divine Person, which was denied by some heretics, is symbolized and confessed. Or, again, the wine represents Christ, and the water, the faithful. This may explain why the celebrant blesses the water, but not the wine. Reflect well on the many useful instructions conveyed in the prayer said during the blessing of the water and its mixture with the wine. At the conclusion of this prayer, the priest, turning, bows to the Cross, showing thereby that he is mindful that the Sacrifice of the Mass is substantially the same as the great offering of the Cross. Having arrived at the middle of the altar, he elevates the chalice, and, with eyes and hands raised toward heaven, makes the oblation in these words: "We offer unto thee, O Lord, the chalice of salvation, beseeching thy clemency that it may ascend before thy divine Majesty as a sweet odor for our salvation, and for that of the whole world. Amen." At the end of this ceremony he makes the sign of the Cross with the chalice, and places it upon the Corporal. Then the thought of his unworthiness seems to rush upon him. Impelled by this salutary thought, he bows down in the attitude of the most humble, fervent prayer, and gives vent to his feelings in the following beautiful appeal: "Accept us, O Lord, in the spirit of humility and contrition of heart; and grant that the Sacrifice which we, this day, offer in thy sight, may be pleasing to thee, O Lord God." After this prayer, the priest, rising, makes the sign of the Cross on the oblation. Whilst doing so, he says: "Come, O Almighty and Eternal God, the Sanctifier, and bless this Sacrifice, prepared for the glory of thy name."

During the moments spent by the priest in uttering these prayers, it is eminently proper for the faithful to enter into the sentiments here called forth — sentiments of humility and contrition. Let them reflect on the incomprehensible majesty of that God to whom alone sacrifice may be offered, and then on their own nothingness. Let them endeavor to acquire more and more correct ideas of the great God and of lowly man. Humility will follow. Then will they exclaim, in the language of the truly humble Psalmist: "What is man, that thou art mindful of him?" (Ps. viii. 5).

Let them also cultivate, at this part of the Mass, sentiments of contrition. Then will they, though lowly and humble, experience that consoling confidence which is founded on the assurance given by the Royal Prophet: "A contrite and humble heart, O God, thou wilt not despise" (Ps. l. 19).

CHAPTER V.

INCENSING—LAVABO—SECRETA.

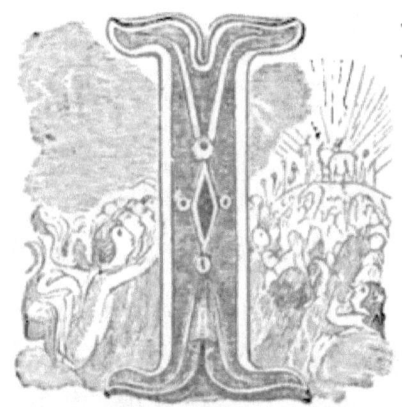

I DEEM it of utility to explain the signification of the rite of incensing, because it conveys important lessons. To the Protestant whom mere curiosity, or, perhaps, a laudable motive leads into the Catholic Church during solemn Mass or Benediction of the most Blessed Sacrament, the ceremony of incensing is, generally, an inexplicable enigma. What means that burning of sweet perfume, that ascending smoke? Were those who are strangers to Catholic rites and ceremonies content with inquiry, we certainly could find no fault with them. They have a right to ask for information, and we are always willing to satisfy such praiseworthy curiosity. But, unfortunately, they too often answer their own query; and the answer which they give is: "It is nothing more or less than another specimen of *Romish* mummery." Not so, respected Protestant brethren. This ceremony has its history and its spiritual, mystical signification. The annals of the Christian Church tell us that there was a time when the Christian people dared not hold their religious assemblies in public, or offer their Sacrifice save in private dwellings, or in those subterranean temples, the catacombs. Then pagan Rome's proud philosophers and jealous priests spared no pains to obtain from the tyrannical Cæsars edicts for the extermination of the disciples of Jesus of Nazareth. Some say that the use of incense, the burning of perfumes in those imperfectly ventilated subterranean places of worship, was a sanitary precaution. Were this natural reason the true and only one, could any sensible man blame the Church for retaining a rite which, whilst in no wise unbecoming, serves to remind the Christians of the nineteenth century of those hard struggles and dire persecutions that compelled his ancestors of the first, second, third, and fourth ages of Christianity to rear their altars and offer their spotless Victim in insalubrious caverns? I do not, however, feel prepared to accept this as the true reason why the burning of perfume was introduced into our solemn offices. It is an undeniable fact that the use of incense in the offices of the Church dates back to the earliest days of Christianity. Does it not carry us to a still more remote period, when the Lord Himself prescribed to the Aaronitic priesthood the use of incense in the sacrifices which they, as His priests, were required to offer to His divine Majesty? Again, does not St. John, in his inimitably grand description of God and of the altar of the Lamb, often speak of the incense offered incessantly in honor of the Eternal (Apoc. viii. 3, 4, 5). The burning of incense has, besides, a mystical, spiritual signification. It is emblematic of prayer. This the same vision-favored disciple tells us. The Psalmist (cxl. 2) regards the ascending of incense as figurative of the prayers of the faithful: "Let my prayer be directed as incense in thy sight." Thus the material perfume burned at the altar in honor of the sacred mysteries is a symbol of that more precious perfume — prayer, which rises from myriads of hearts in which the fire of the love of God burns. The prayers said by the priest whilst performing this ceremony of incensing are expressive of this spiritual signification. Whilst giving this explanation to our

Protestant brethren, in answer to their inquiry, and in refutation of their hasty, rash, and unjust condemnation of this liturgical practice, let me earnestly invite the children of the Church to profit by a ceremony so replete with instruction. Reflect how high and holy is that altar, how sacred the offerings, and how worthy of respect and veneration are all those persons and objects incensed during the august Sacrifice.

Immediately after the incensing, which takes place only in solemn Masses, the priest repairs to the Epistle side of the altar for the Lavabo, or washing of his hands. The prayer said during this act is found in Psalm xxv. verses 6, 7, 8, 9, 10, 11, 12. There was in the earlier ages of the Church, when the officiating minister receives the offerings of the faithful, an especial propriety in purifying his hands after having handled so many offerings. The spiritual signification is worthy of our notice. This ceremony readily conveys to the Christian mind exalted ideas of that purity of heart and hand that should adorn the Christian ministers at the Eucharistic table. It also reminds those assisting at the Sacrifice, how sinless and pure they should be.

Upon his return to the middle of the altar, we notice the priest bowed down most reverently. He is saying another prayer, in which he again offers the holy Sacrifice to God. He begs the holy Triune God to accept the oblation, that it may be to the glory of God, to the honor of the saints, and conducive to the salvation of the entire faithful people. The prayer is as follows: "Receive, O holy Trinity, this oblation, which we make to thee in memory of the Passion, Resurrection, and Ascension of our Lord Jesus Christ, and in honor of the blessed Mary ever virgin, of blessed John the

Baptist, the holy Apostles Peter and Paul, and of all the saints; that it may be available to their honor and our salvation; and may they vouchsafe to intercede for us in heaven, whose memory we celebrate on earth. Through the same Christ our Lord. Amen." He is now drawing near the most solemn part of the Mass—that in which the Consecration is to take place. He feels the awful solemnity of the moment; he trembles at the more than angelic function which he is soon to perform; he distrusts himself; bows down, kisses the altar, and, turning to the people, says aloud: "Brethren, pray that my Sacrifice and yours may be acceptable to God the Father Almighty." The clerk, in the name of the assembled faithful, says: "May the Lord receive the Sacrifice from thy hands, to the praise and glory of his name, to our benefit, and to that of all His holy Church." The priest's invitation to the people is a most earnest appeal. It should be responded to with all that heartfelt fervor and holy earnestness which invariably cause the petitions of even poor imperfect men to ascend to heaven and reach the throne of the Most High. Tepidity in our response to this appeal would be entirely unbecoming. We may feel that our poor prayers can avail but little. We should, notwithstanding this feeling, pray with all earnestness. Perhaps our supplications may be, like those of the poor publican, at once hearkened to by Him who exalts the humble. Besides, the prayer of the entire Christian flock may, by the holy violence offered to heaven, effect what individual appeals would never have been able to accomplish. The priest, having turned to the altar, is engaged in silent, secret prayer. Hence these prayers have been called "Secreta," or secret.

These supplications may be considered the immediate preparation for the "Canon" of the Mass.

Have those who see in the Mass nothing but meaningless robes, and unintelligible language, and ridiculous ceremonies, ever adverted to the fact that this sacred function, even considered apart from the essence of the Sacrifice itself, is one continued series of admirable prayers? Is the Catholic Christian fully impressed that the time of Mass is, by excellence, the time of prayer? If so, why do we sometimes find not a few who appear to be at a loss what to do or how to occupy themselves while assisting at Mass? Follow the priest in the various prayers and ceremonies for the oblation of the great Eucharistic Sacrifice, and your time will not be a burden to you. On the contrary, you will find it too short! Your difficulty will be, how to crowd so many acts of devotion, so many earnest supplications, into the half hour usually required for the celebration of the Holy Mass.

CHAPTER VI.

PREFACE AND SANCTUS.

HE Preface and Sanctus, which form the subject of this chapter, introduce us into the Canon — the most solemn part of the sacred liturgy. The word Preface signifies introduction. Those assisting at Mass will remark that it is said in a *loud* voice, and is evidently addressed to the faithful assembled around the altar. The first words of the Preface are: "Per omnia sæcula sæculorum"—"World without end." This is the conclusion of the secret prayers spoken of in the preceding chapter.

Silence prevailed during the "Secreta." That silence is now broken. To the "World without end," the whole congregation, by their representative, answer: "Amen." Then the priest addresses the faithful in that beautiful and appropriate salutation, "Dominus vobiscum" —"The Lord be with you," to which the usual answer is made, "And with thy spirit." You will notice that, in this instance, the priest, in saluting the faithful, does not turn toward them. Having the oblations before him, and his whole mind centered on the great work in which he is engaged, the celebrant is unwilling to turn away from the altar, or in any manner divert his attention.

In the earlier ages of the Church, the officiating priest was from the beginning of the Preface entirely separated from the congregation by means of a large veil or curtain, dropped or drawn at that point of the liturgy, and not raised or removed till after the Consecration. The mystery of the unbloody renewal of Calvary's Sacrifice was consummated in a silence and solitude resembling that which reigned within the Holy of Holies in God's temple of old. This separation no longer exists in the Latin Church; but, even now, she wishes her minister at the altar to remember that, at this part of the Mass, he stands on holier ground, and that he is the minister of God in a more exalted sense than was the high-priest among the Jewish people. From this hallowed spot and in this exalted position he raises his voice and bids the Christian people prepare in earnest for the most solemn act of Consecration. This he does by inviting them to elevate their hearts from earth to heaven, from creatures to God. "Sursum corda" —"Raise your hearts," says he, in a loud voice. Raise your hearts, because, in a few moments, you are to unite your praises with those chanted, before the throne of the Lamb by myriads of adoring, celestial spirits; raise your hearts, because you are to assist at sublime mysteries far above human sense and comprehension. Fully convinced of the propriety, nay, of the necessity, of attending to this most opportune invitation, the entire assembly of the faithful, by the mouth of their representative, the clerk, answer: " Habemus ad Dominum" —"We have them raised to the Lord." Would to God that this assurance given by the people were always literally true in the case of each individual assisting at the Sacrifice. Then, indeed, would they be in proper dispositions to reap that plenitude of blessings which the Eucharistic Sacrifice was intended to convey; then, indeed, would that sloth, indifference, and listlessness which are, alas! too often noticeable, even during this most important part of the liturgy, entirely cease; then, indeed, would the spectacle of the faithful worshiping at the Christian altar, be one upon which the very angels might look down with complacency.

Supposing all hearts raised to the Lord, the priest, with eyes, and hands, and heart uplifted to the Cross, again, in a loud voice, says: "Gratias agamus Domino Deo nostro"—"Let us render thanks to the Lord our God;" to which invitation those serving respond: "Dignum et justum est"—"It is meet and just." Yes, Christian reader, if ever it is meet and just and highly becoming to render thanks the most earnest to the Lord our God, it is at this time, when the Eucharistic mystery—the mystery of Jesus' greatest love for us—is about to be renewed in the miracle of transubstantiation. It being, therefore, admitted that it is in the highest degree proper to praise and thank the Lord our God, the priest, with whom the people ought to unite, continues the Preface in these words: "It is truly meet and just, right and available to salvation, that we should always, and in all places, give thanks to thee, O Holy Lord, Father Almighty, Eternal God, through Christ our Lord, by whom the Angels praise thy majesty; the Dominations adore it; the Powers tremble before it; the heavenly Virtues and blessed Seraphim, with common jubilee, glorify it. Together with whom, we beseech Thee, that we may be admitted to join our humble voices, saying: "Holy, holy, holy, Lord God of Sabaoth! heaven and earth are full of thy glory! Hozanna in the highest! Blessed is he that cometh in the name of the Lord! Hozanna in the highest!" What more beautiful expression of thanksgiving? Poor, frail mortals uniting their humble voices with the celestial choirs! What more affecting—what more solemn or more sublime prayer! what, in a word, more suitable to impress the faithful with the highest ideas of the majesty of the God whom we adore? At the end of the Preface, during the words, "Holy, holy, holy," etc., the priest bows down in the attitude of profound adoration.

This canticle of praise and adoration is borrowed from heaven. It is the celestial song which the visioned-favored Isaias heard the seraphim incessantly chanting before the throne of the Deity. (Isaias vi. 3). It is the strain in which the beloved disciple heard the four living creatures giving glory, and honor, and benediction to Him that sitteth upon the throne, who liveth for ever and ever: "And they rested not day and night, saying: Holy, holy, holy, Lord God Almighty, who was, who is, and who is to come" (Apoc. iv. 8, 9). By means of it, how beautifully do earth and heaven, men and angels, the Church triumphant and the Church militant, blend their voices in one common hymn of praise to their one common Lord and God! In it man, notwithstanding his lowliness and frailties, seems to rise to the level of angels, and to partake of the seraphic fires—the love of God, kindled and kept alive by the God of love. Thrice is the Sanctus, or Holy, said in honor of the three divine Persons of the Godhead. The last words of the canticle are: "Blessed is he that cometh in the name of the Lord. Hozanna in the highest." These words are taken from the New Testament (Matt. xxi. 9), and were addressed by the Jews to our Saviour on the occasion of his triumphant entry into Jerusalem, a few days before his Passion. If by the exclamation, "Holy, holy, holy!" we testified our faith in Jesus Christ as one of the divine Persons, as God, by these last words we profess our faith in the mystery of the Incarnation in which he was made man, and appeared among us. Hozanna is an expression of joy and exultation.

In solemn Masses this canticle is sung by the priest. There is in the chant, when properly executed, something truly grand—eminently calculated to inspire devotion. On certain solemnities, and at certain seasons of the ecclesiastical year, a few words expressive of the mystery commemorated are introduced into the Preface. At the words, "Blessed is he that cometh in the name of the Lord," the priest signs himself with the sign of the Cross. This ceremony should remind the faithful that if they may, now, utter the hozanna of joy and exultation, all thanks are due to the mystery of the Cross, for without this consoling event we would have been doomed life-long, like the captive Jews by the rivers of Babylon, always to exclaim: "How shall we sing the song of the Lord in a strange land!" (Ps. cxxxv. 4).

Such is the Preface to the most solemn part of the Mass—a preface worthy of what follow, and expressive, as far as human language can be, of a mystery truly divine! We are invited to prepare for the Canon of the Mass. The mode of preparation is indicated. All that the writer desires is, to make known the wish of the Church, and, for the glory of God and our own interests, to urge compliance with that wish of our most tender Mother.

CHAPTER VII.

CANON.

THIS part of the Mass has, at all times, been regarded as the most solemn, because in it is performed the mysterious act of Consecration, by which, through the ministry of the priest, and in virtue of the almighty power of God, and the words of Jesus Christ, the substance of the material elements — bread and wine — is changed into the true and real body and blood of the Incarnate Son of God.

In approaching the subject, the most gifted mind may well confess its inability to do justice to the divine mysteries here consummated, or even to the sublime liturgy prescribed by the Church for their celebration. So solemn is this part of the Mass, that every ceremony which the priest performs, every prayer which he utters, and every aspiration of his heart, tends to it as to its center — clusters around it, and receives therefrom its significance. So solemn is it, that whilst other parts of the Mass varied to some extent, in different countries and churches, this part — the Canon — is substantially the same as it was in the days of St. Chrysostom and St. Augustine. Hence the name Canon, which signifies rule or fixed rule.

What must have been noticed by the faithful is, that most of the Canon — the prayers preceding, accompanying, and a great portion of those following the act of Consecration — are said in so *low* a voice as not to be audible to the assisting people. As far as it is now ascertainable, this has been at all times the custom.

What motive could the Church have had for prescribing that this portion of the Mass, so edifying in the ceremonial, so affecting in the prayers, so sublime in the mysteries consummated, should be said by her minister in a *low* voice? As Catholics, it is well for us to know that the Church has anathematized those who condemn this ordinance (Council of Trent, Sess. xxii. Can. 9). In answer, however, to our inquiry, we have the words of that same venerable authority: "And whereas such is the nature of man, that without external helps he cannot easily be raised to meditation on divine things, therefore has holy Mother Church instituted certain rites, to wit: that certain things be pronounced in the Mass in a low voice, and others in a louder tone" (Sess. xxii. chap. 5). With this authoritative assurance of the Church, that this rite was ordained to assist the faithful in their "meditation on divine things," is it not surprising, and painful too, to find those who are hostile to the Catholic Church assigning the most unbecoming, nay, sinister, motives or reasons for this liturgical prescription? Some have asserted that the Church prescribed the reading of this part of the Mass *in a low* voice in order to keep the faithful in ignorance of what transpires. Such a charge could not have been made in good faith. Have those who assail the motives which actuate the Church taken the necessary pains to obtain that amount of information without which their judgment is *rash* and almost invariably *incorrect* and *unjust?* The same rash and unjust charge is made concerning the disciplinary legislation by which the Church has required her pastors to use the Latin language in the sacred liturgy.

It is affirmed that this practice is unreasonable in itself, and, in its consequences, injurious to the people. We, on the contrary, maintain that she had and still has good reasons for deciding that it is inexpedient to use the vernacular tongue in the Mass. The Church adopted the Latin as the language of her liturgy at a time when that language was spoken by the greatest part of the civilized world—the Roman Empire. She continued to use it, even when the Latin ceased to be a living, spoken language, for the following good reasons: "1. She considers a language no longer undergoing changes as best suited for the celebration of mysteries and the administration of sacraments in which the faith that changeth not is conveyed. 2. The preservation of a common language in our common service, tends to preserve and strengthen the extended union of her holy brotherhood. 3. It enables her clergy to officiate at every altar, and makes her laity find a home in every church of her communion. 4. All tongues and tribes and nations are thus united together, and become one people, adoring one common Father, grateful to one common Redeemer, and beseeching sanctification from one Holy Spirit. 5. Moreover, this salutary discipline unites ages as it binds nations, for the liturgy which we use has descended to us from the primitive days of our religion. The very words in which an Ambrose and an Augustine officiated, whose substance they received from apostolic men, being now repeated at our altars." We further maintain that no injury is done the people, for whatever the officiating minister at the altar says in the Latin language, they may possess in their own tongue—faithful translations of the liturgy, and books with appropriate prayers, being allowed by the Church.

In the case of the Canon, I will assign a reason for silence, or for a low voice, akin to that given by the Council of Trent—a certain propriety which exists. In the prophecy of Habacuc, chapter ii. verse 20, we read: "But the Lord is in his holy temple, let all the earth keep silence before him." Now, if silence was recommended by the inspired prophet as suitable in the presence of God, why may not the divinely commissioned Church of Christ prescribe silence, or rather a low, inaudible voice, as becoming in that part of her sacred liturgy in which the awe-inspiring Sacrifice of Calvary's mountain is renewed and commemorated? Again, the whole mystery of the Eucharist is so exalted, so far transcending human or angelic comprehension, so absolutely beyond the reach of our senses, that all is effected by the secret, invisible operation of the Omnipotent. Now, does not the Church, by the low voice prescribed for the Canon, enter most beautifully into the very spirit and nature of the mystery? Silence excites and nourishes piety. This hardly requires proof. Experience establishes beyond question that, that "meditation on divine things," to which the Church wishes to elevate the hearts of her children, is wonderfully facilitated by silence and solitude. If so, can we conceive any circumstances in which the aids to heartfelt piety and earnest meditation are more opportunely brought into requisition, than in the Canon of the Mass, during which the faithful are called upon to apply every faculty of the mind and every affection of the heart to meditation on a mystery truly divine.

During this most solemn part of the Mass, the priest has his hands uplifted and outstretched, to express the elevation of his heart to Heaven. The spirit of dissipation is entirely out of place during the Canon. If distractions, wilfully consented to during prayer, are, under any circumstance, an insult to the thrice holy God, with whom we are graciously permitted to hold sweet converse, does it not assume a peculiar malignity when we are engaged in the highest act of worship, in offering to our Maker that tremendous Sacrifice upon which the blessed spirits look down with holy awe and reverence?

Since, then, the want of that attention and reverence is a painful evidence of the absence of faith and fervid charity, we should renew our *faith*, cultivate that virtue which will enable us to appreciate that which divine Wisdom has seen fit to conceal from mortal eyes— the consoling realities contained in the great Eucharistic Sacrifice. We should also apply to the attainment of that other essential virtue, charity, by which alone we will have it in our power to render to the hidden God of the Eucharistic tabernacle, a suitable return for that mystery of an Incarnate God's greatest love.

CHAPTER VIII.

CANON (CONTINUED)—PRAYERS AND CEREMONIES PRECEDING THE CONSECRATION.

THE prayers and ceremonies of the Canon may be divided into three parts—namely, those preceding the act of Consecration; those accompanying it; or the words of Consecration, and those that follow it.

As soon as the priest has finished the magnificent Preface or introduction to the Canon, raising his eyes and hands toward heaven, he, as it were, expresses his eager desire to hasten the descent of Jesus Christ upon the altar. Then, joining his hands and bowing down in the attitude of supplication, he begins the following beautiful and expressive prayer: "We, therefore, humbly pray and beseech thee, most merciful Father, through Jesus Christ, thy Son, our Lord, that thou wouldst vouchsafe to accept and bless these ✣ gifts, these ✣ presents, these ✣ holy, unspotted sacrifices, which, in the first place, we offer thee for the holy Catholic Church, to which vouchsafe to grant peace; as also to preserve, unite, and govern it throughout the world; together with thy servant N. our Pope, N. our Bishop, as also all orthodox believers and professors of the Catholic and apostolic faith." The word *therefore* shows that this first prayer of the Canon is intimately connected with that canticle of homage—the Preface: "We *humbly* pray and beseech thee, most merciful Father." In the use of the word *humbly*, the Church teaches us the necessity of humility in our appeal to the throne of grace. She seems to direct our attention to the lesson conveyed by the inspired writer of Ecclesiasticus: "The prayer of him that humbleth himself shall pierce the clouds" (xxxv. 21). *Pray* and *beseech* are not synonymous words. To *pray* is simply to ask, to petition; to *beseech* is to supplicate earnestly or strongly. The latter, besides the idea of asking, implies importuning. Her earnest prayers and importunings are uttered with a well-founded confidence, because addressed to a *Father*, and not merely to a Father, but to a *most merciful* Father. Yet, while adverting to the fact that the heavenly Father's mercy is "from eternity and unto eternity upon them that fear him" (Ps. cii. 17), still, knowing how, as children of wrath, we have no claims on that consoling attribute, except through the

Redeemer, she adds: "Through Jesus Christ, thy Son, our Lord."

For what does the Church supplicate? That the most merciful Father would vouchsafe to bless and accept the gifts, presents, and holy, unspotted sacrifices which she offers. For whom does she make these offerings? In the first place, for the holy Catholic Church, the Spouse of Jesus Christ, by whom the merciful Father begets his children. She *alone*, as a *holy* Church, has a right to participate in the Sacrifice to the thrice holy God. All others claiming to be *holy* Churches are but unhallowed assemblies, without a divine Founder. What are the blessings humbly asked for in behalf of the holy Catholic Church? *Peace* —that peace which her Founder wished the Apostles and Disciples; *preservation*, in order that she may continue the noble work entrusted to her—the announcement of the glad tidings of salvation to all nations; *unity*, by which she may be ever faithful to keep intact the inestimable deposit of divine revelation, and a *unity* of government by which she may be always distinguishable from the *headless*, discordant, and jarring sects constantly springing up around her.

In the next place, prayer is offered for him who is seated in the chair of Peter, the Sovereign Pontiff, the visible Head of the Church and Vicar of Jesus Christ, in order that he may, at all times, prove himself a vigilant sentinel, ever ready to sound the alarm when the wolf in sheep's clothing approaches the fold of Christ. Afterwards those appointed by the Holy Ghost to rule the Church of God — subordinately to the Sovereign Pontiff — the bishops, are remembered. In fine, she supplicates for all those who are her children by orthodox faith. How admirably comprehensive is this prayer of the Canon! How replete

OF THE MASS. 155

with useful instruction for the faithful assembled around the Eucharistic altar! The order in which supplication is made is worthy of our attention.

Immediately after this general prayer, the priest raises his hands and holds them joined before his breast, while making a special memento of those for whom he intends to pray in particular. This memento of the living is made as follows: "Be mindful, O Lord, of thy servants, men and women, N. and N;" then, continuing his prayer, he says, "and of all here present, whose faith and devotion are known to thee; for whom we offer up to thee, or who offer up to thee, this sacrifice of praise for themselves, their families and friends; for the redemption of their souls, for the health and salvation they hope for, and for which they now pay their vows to thee, eternal, living and true God." Whilst the priest is thus engaged, the faithful, in order to enter into the designs of the Church, ought to pray most fervently in behalf of those for whom they are in any way particularly obliged to supplicate. Here the parent may, very appropriately, appeal to the God of all blessings in favor of the child; and children, with all the earnestness prompted by filial affection and sense of duty, for parents. Here, also, our benefactors in the spiritual and temporal order should be recommended to the mercy of God. Notice that the priest prays particularly for all *present* at the holy Sacrifice. Do those who, through spiritual sloth, assist so seldom at Mass ever advert to the many graces which they might obtain in virtue of the commemoration here made? Remark, moreover, that it is for such as are present with *faith* and *devotion* the Church prays. What is asked? The redemption of their souls—the most important of all affairs; for " what doth it profit a man if he gain the whole world and suffer the loss of his own soul? Or what exchange shall a man give for his soul?" (Matt. xvi. 26). After the great spiritual goods, temporal blessings are prayed for—health with concomitant and consequent blessings. This prayer being ended, the priest proceeds to the following: "Communicating with and honoring, in the first place, the memory of the ever-glorious Virgin Mary, Mother of our Lord and God, Jesus Christ, as also of the blessed Apostles and Martyrs Peter and Paul, Andrew, James, John, Thomas, James, Philip, Bartholomew, Matthew, Simon and Thaddeus, Linus, Cletus, Clement, Xixtus, Cornelius, Cyprian, Lawrence, Chrysogony, John and Paul, Cosmas and Damian, and of all thy saints; by whose merits and prayers, grant that we may be always defended by the help of thy protection. Through the same Christ, our Lord. Amen."

In this prayer of the liturgy, the Church directs our attention to that consoling article of our faith, the "Communion of Saints," which consists in the union of the three parts of the mystical body of Jesus Christ—those in heaven, or the Church triumphant; those on earth, or the Church militant; and those in purgatory. She reminds us that this union does not consist merely in being all members of the same family, but likewise in the right which those in heaven have to our homage of respect and veneration, and in the assurance which faith gives us of the lawfulness and utility of their intercession.

Among those blessed servants of the living and true God, she would have us honor first of all the ever-blessed Virgin, the most exalted of those worshiping before the throne of God; then the holy

Apostles, who were our teachers in that divine law which they received from the lips of Jesus Himself. With the Apostles she associates the holy Martyrs who, by the shedding of their blood, sealed and confirmed the faith which they had received from those divinely commissioned teachers. In fine, as it would be next to impossible to enumerate all her saints, she adds the invocation of all her triumphant children. Toward the conclusion of this prayer, she places before our eyes the end and object of this invocation, by soliciting help and protection through their merits and prayers.

In this prayer, the doctrine of the Church in regard to the invocation of the blessed in heaven, is set forth in such manner as ought to suffice to silence the adversaries of this teaching. It is simply their *intercession* that we invoke! It is their sanctity—a participation in God's holiness—that we honor! Is there aught in this teaching derogatory to the honor and glory due to the all-holy and all-powerful God, or injurious to the Incarnate Word as the great sole Mediator of the New Law?

The next prayer of the Canon begins with the word "Hanc igitur." It is more immediately preparatory to the Consecration, and implores God to accept the oblation and sacrifice. During it the priest holds his hands spread out over the bread and wine. This ceremony, prescribed by the Almighty to the priests of the Jewish Dispensation, in the oblation of the victim (Levit. i. 4), signifies that the offering upon which hands are imposed holds the place of the offerer, who, by his sins, merited to be himself immolated to the anger of the most just God. The ceremony retains all its significance in the Mass, or great Eucharistic Sacrifice. The priest, in the name of the entire Church, makes the oblation, and, by imposing his hands, signifies that Jesus Christ, into whose body and blood the material oblation is soon to be converted, is the Victim of propitiation now offered to the eternal Father. We sinners were the culprits upon whom his wrath would have fallen had not this most merciful Redeemer assumed the debt. But "he was wounded for our iniquities; he was bruised for our sins; and the chastisement of our peace was upon him, and by his bruises we are healed" (Isaias liii. 5). The prayer "Hanc igitur" is as follows: "We therefore beseech thee, O Lord, graciously to accept the oblation of our servitude, as also of thy whole family; dispose our days in thy peace, preserve us from eternal damnation, and rank us in the number of thy elect. Through Christ our Lord. Amen."

Is there not ample subject of reflection the most useful in the petitions here made? Is not this moment, in which the greatest mystery of divine love is to be consummated, of all the most appropriate for the utterance of such petitions? Ponder well and seriously on the words and spirit of the various prayers of the Canon. Let the heart feel what the lips express.

CHAPTER IX.

WORDS OF THE PROMISE.

IN the explanation of the prayers and ceremonies of the Mass, I have arrived at the solemn, mysterious act of Consecration, by which the material elements of bread and wine are, by the Almighty power of God, converted *truly*, *really*, and *substantially* into the body and blood of Jesus Christ.

As the doctrine of the Catholic Church on this mystery of the Real Presence is so important, and yet so imperfectly understood by our separated brethren, I deem it expedient to devote considerable space to the treatment of this subject, even at the risk of interrupting to some extent the moral and liturgical reflections. Of course, in a work of this nature, a full development of these proofs is not looked for. Enough, however, will be said to show the grounds of the Catholic faith in the holy Eucharist, and the futility of the various objections made against that faith. Though keenly sensible of the wrong done us in the sneer, ridicule, and smile of contempt with which we are taunted on account of this article of our belief, still, we are ever ready with true charity to utter words of heartfelt prayer for those who misrepresent us, and, most of all, our holy and dear faith: "Father, forgive them, for they know not what they do" (Luke xxiii. 34).

This chapter will establish the fact, that Jesus Christ did *promise* to leave us his true and real body and blood for

the food and nourishment of our souls.*
Christian reader, take your New Testament and peruse attentively the sixth chapter of the Gospel according to St. John. You cannot fail to notice in it three distinct things: 1. A miracle—the multiplication of the five loaves; 2. A discourse on faith, in which this virtue is recommended in very strong terms; 3. A great number of verses on eating his flesh and drinking his blood. Do you think that our Saviour's discourse contained those three things *without a design?* Or can you imagine that the inspired writer penned them *without a motive?* By no means! They are intimately connected, and they tend admirably to establish the point in question: namely, that Jesus Christ *did promise* to leave us his true and real body in

---

* The Scriptural proofs of the Real Presence are taken substantially, and, in some instances, verbatim, from Rev. Dr. Fredet's excellent treatise, "Eucharistic Mystery."

the holy Eucharist to be our nourishment.

In the first place, a miracle is wrought. God never works such wonders without having a suitable object in view.

If we examine the sixth chapter of St. John to ascertain the object which He had in view in this instance, the impartial inquirer will, I think, see at once that it was to prove that He was the *Almighty God*, and, this point established, that He had a right to their faith, no matter how incomprehensible the revelation He might see fit to make unto them.

In the second place, He discourses on faith. A question presents itself: Why did He in this case, and at this particular time, insist so strongly on the necessity of faith? We are irresistibly led to conclude that He was preparing the minds of His audience for some important revelation which none save the *Om-*

nipotent God could make, and none save those imbued with divine faith could accept.

Such being the case, it behooves us now to consider what this important revelation was. Jesus Christ Himself gives us the answer in the 51st and 52d verses: "*I am the living bread which came down from heaven. If any man eat of this bread, he shall live for ever; and the bread that I will give is my flesh, for the life of the world.*" What do these words mean? Here a most serious disagreement exists between the Catholic Church and the various denominations of Protestantism which sprang up in the sixteenth century, and subsequently. The former—the Catholic Church—that Church which the great Apostle St. Paul termed "the pillar and ground of truth" (1 Tim. iii. 15), has always taught that Jesus Christ *promised* His true and real body and blood for the life of the world. The latter—at least such of the Protestant denominations as admit the Eucharist in any sense—teach that Jesus promised only a *figure* or *symbol* of His body and blood. This most serious difference is on a point of incalculable importance—a point upon which, according to our divine Saviour, life eternal depends: "Amen, amen, I say to you, Except you eat the flesh of the Son of man, and drink his blood, you shall not have life in you" (St. John vi. 54).

The subject is, therefore, entitled to the dispassionate and impartial investigation of every Christian who has any regard for eternal life. In order to facilitate this investigation as to the true meaning of the words of Christ, I will lay before you the reasons which the Catholic Church assigns for having taken the words of the Saviour in the *literal*, and not in the *figurative* sense—in the sense of a *true* and *real* presence, and not in that of a *symbolical* and *figurative* presence.

She adopts as a rule for the interpretation of the sacred Scriptures, that every text must be taken in the literal — in that sense which it obviously and naturally conveys, unless there exist a reason for construing it otherwise. Now, no one can deny that the words of the *promise* of the holy Eucharist *in themselves* are clear and positive in the sense of a real presence. If there existed any doubt as to the true import of His words, certainly we can desire no better exponents than those who stood around Jesus, and heard these words as they fell from His divine lips. Well; it is a fact that the Jews whom Christ addressed understood Him to speak of His real flesh, else to what purpose their question: "How can this man give us his flesh to eat?" (verse 53). But may they not have misunderstood Him? Not at all; for when they strove among themselves and asked the question, Jesus perceived their embarrassment, and saw distinctly what meaning they attached to His words. If they misunderstood Him, was He not bound to correct their mistake? This He was accustomed to do. Did He do so—did He explain? On the contrary, He only confirmed, in stronger language, what He had a moment before said: "Amen, amen, I say to you, Except you eat the flesh of the Son of man, and drink his blood, you shall not have life in you" (verse 54). Can language be stronger, more explicit, more expressive of the promise of a *real presence?* On the other hand, what language more delusive, more apt to lead His audience into error, if He meant only a *figurative presence?*

Weigh well this reason for our belief that the holy Eucharist contains, *truly, really* and *substantially*, the body and blood of Jesus Christ, and add to it the reasons furnished by the following circumstances: 1. He prefaces this discourse on the holy Eucharistic mystery with a miracle. To what purpose this miracle? Is any such prodigy necessary for the institution of empty memorials? — to command our faith that what was bread and wine still remains the same? 2. He promised a bread from heaven — a bread superior to that which their fathers did eat in the desert — to the manna. If Jesus Christ meant only ordinary bread, figurative, if you will, of His body and blood, where is its superiority over the manna, which was, in its origin and effects, *more* than ordinary bread? Where is its heavenly quality? 3. The Jews are scandalized; so are the disciples. They walk no more with Him. They are scandalized because they understood Him to speak of a *real* eating of His real and true body. Does He modify, explain, or recall His words? Far from it. He is willing to let even His Apostles go away: "Will you also go away?" (verse 68). Is it not evident that they did not misunderstand Him?

But the advocates of the *figurative* sense will not permit us to triumph so easily. They tell us that Christ did explain His words as follows: "It is the spirit that quickeneth; the flesh profiteth nothing" (verse 64). As an explanation of the difficulty, this text is inadmissible for two reasons: 1. I suppose we dare not put in the mouth of Jesus Christ a language unworthy of a sensible man. Jesus, a moment before, had said that His flesh did profit: "He that eateth my flesh, and drinketh my blood, hath everlasting life." Can He now, a moment later, in the same discourse, and upon the same subject, say that His flesh profiteth nothing? He cannot. He does not say, *my* flesh, but *the* flesh; that is their carnal manner of understanding, whereby they failed to apprehend that it was of a sacramental reception of His body and blood He spoke. 2. We cannot admit this text as an explanation, because if the Saviour had intended and offered it as such, in the Protestant sense, certainly it would have removed all cause of complaint and murmur. But if you will again refer to the sixth chapter of St. John's Gospel, you will find that it was after this would-be explanation that the disciples went back and walked no more with Him (verse 67.) It was then also that Jesus asked His Apostles whether they too would leave Him? (verse 68), to which Simon Peter, in the name of the rest, replied: " Lord, to whom shall we go? thou hast the words of eternal life" (verse 69). Thus we see that this text, instead of being an explanation, in the sense attached to it by non-Catholics, is another powerful proof of the doctrine of the Real Presence.

Such are the Scriptural reasons upon which the Church grounds her belief that a true and real presence was intended and promised. Those who differ from us in this point of faith have not, after three hundred years of effort, been able to assign any reason to the contrary sufficient to convince her, or any honest inquirer after truth, that she is wrong. They have, it is true, like the Jews and the apostate disciples, vauntingly asked: "How can this man give us his flesh to eat?" Their condition is worse than that of the unbelieving Jews, for these said, "How can this *man?*" and those believing the Divinity of Jesus Christ must say, "How can this *God-man* give us his flesh to eat?" The Catholic Church, however, answers them in the language of Jesus Christ: "Except you eat the flesh of the Son of man, and drink his blood, you shall not have life in you." They also call this doctrine *hard*—hard to be believed; and they will not hear the Church commissioned by Jesus to teach all truth, even to the consummation of the world. So thought the Jews, and so they acted in leaving Christ, simply because He saw fit to reveal or to promise a doctrine impervious to human reason. The Catholic Church, and every Catholic, admits that this dogma transcends all human or created understanding, but with Peter, the Prince of the Apostles, we exclaim: "Lord, to whom shall we go? thou hast the words of eternal life."

CHAPTER X.

WORDS OF THE INSTITUTION.

THE fulfillment of the promise spoken of in the preceding chapter is found in St. Matthew xxvi. 26, 27, 28, and in words substantially the same in St. Mark xiv. 22, 23, 24; St. Luke xxii. 19, 20; and in 1 Cor. xi. 23, 24, 25.

Though the words in which our blessed Redeemer promised the holy Eucharist are amply sufficient to establish the Real Presence, still the texts above indicated furnish other powerful, overwhelming proofs of the same point of doctrine. It is evident, and will be admitted by all, that the words of the Institution, "This is my body," etc., prove a Real Presence if they are to be understood, not in the figurative, but in the literal sense, as held by Catholics. Now, that they are to be understood in the literal sense, is equally evident from many forcible considerations. I will propose the following for your serious reflection:

I. The object which the Saviour had in view in the institution of the holy Eucharist was to reveal a *new article of faith*—to institute *a sacrament*, to *enact a law*, and to make his *te tament*, or *last will*. Now, all these things should be expressed in plain words. Dogmas, articles of faith, must be conveyed in plain and unmistakable terms. If not, they become an occasion of error for the sincere Christian. This should be the case especially in the opinion of Protestants, who admit no rule of faith, except the Bible. Sacraments being intended for the general use and advantage of the faithful, must contain nothing in the words of the institution that could leave erroneous impressions on the Christian mind. Jesus *enacted a law:* "Amen, amen, I say to you, Except you eat the flesh of the Son of man, and drank his blood, you shall not have life in you." Now, wise and prudent legislators do not couch their enactments in metaphorical or ambiguous language. Can we attribute less wisdom, less prudence or precaution, to the Lawgiver of Christianity than we accord to men? Jesus was making His last will or testament. Is there any important action in which men are more careful to eschew figurative and obscure language? Could less be expected of the divine Testator?

II. The circumstances attending the institution of the holy Eucharist also require unambiguous language. When did it take place? The evening before his death. What manner of speech became so solemn a moment? Do men on such occasions express themselves *figuratively* and ambiguously? To whom were the words in question addressed? To his cherished Apostles, to his faithful disciples. Is it possible that Christ would have spoken in figurative terms, or that He would have expressly mentioned the giving of His *body* and *blood*, if He meant only the figure of both? Such a course would most unquestionably have been calculated to deceive those docile and illiterate men. To others, He at times spoke in parables, but to them, clearly.

III. The rules of Biblical criticism require the words of the sacred Scripture to be taken in their literal signification. St. Augustine's rule in regard to the interpretation of the Scripture is, that the words of Holy Writ must always be taken in their proper and obvious signification, unless other and clearer texts, or some evident and incontestable reasons require a different meaning. We confidently challenge the opponents of the literal sense to point out any other and clearer texts, requiring the abandonment of the literal and the adoption of the figurative sense. Where are the "evident and incontestable reasons" requiring Christians to reject the literal, and replace it by a figurative interpretation? There is nothing in the doctrine of the Real Presence repugnant or perplexing to the mind of the sincere Christian. Every thing connected with the mystery is worthy of the omnipotence, wisdom, and ineffable goodness of the Redeemer. Is it alleged that the mystery is impossible?—"How can this man give us his flesh to eat?" The true and well-instructed Christian smiles at the simplicity of those who talk about impossibilities when it is question of the institutions of the Omnipotent God. Is it said that the mystery of the Real Presence presents to our understanding insuperable difficulties? The true and well-instructed Christian fails to discover any greater difficulty in this mystery than in those of the Trinity, Incarnation, or Redemption. The Catholic Church reminds those who reject the doctrine of the Real Presence on the ground of incomprehensibility, that, to be consistent, they should also deny the mystery of a God dying an ignominious death on the Cross, the mystery too of the second adorable Person of the Trinity assuming human nature. She clearly perceives that the Protestant principle, logically carried out, would involve the rejection of the entire Christian faith, based as that faith is on a few incomprehensible, fundamental mysteries.

IV. To give the words of the institution of the holy Eucharist a metaphorical sense, violence must be done to the ordinary rules of human language. This is clearly pointed out by those whose professed object it is to enter into the details of these proofs.

V. The very tenor of the Saviour's discourse, and the whole context, the plainness and force of His expressions, inevitably compel us to admit that He meant His words to be taken in the literal and obvious sense. Read the words and reflect upon them, and you will become more and more satisfied that they convey the doctrine of the Real Presence, and cannot be made to mean any thing else, except by an unwarrantable violence to language, which common sense condemns.

Were the foregoing considerations to leave any doubt in the mind of the sincere inquirer after truth, St. Paul steps forward to add his testimony. He is an important witness, testifying to the true sense of the words in question. He was not with the Apostles when Jesus instituted the holy Eucharist, being then a zealous Pharisee, and soon after a violent persecutor of the Christian Church. What is the testimony of this great Apostle? You will find it in the eleventh chapter of the First Corinthians. He tells us that he received from the Lord Jesus that which he also delivers in regard to the Eucharist—the body and blood of the Lord. He gives *substantially* the same words of institution as the three Evangelists—adding, however, other words calculated to remove all doubt as to the sense of the words of the institution. He says: "For as often as you shall eat this bread and drink the chalice, you shall shew forth the death of the Lord until he come. Therefore, whosoever shall eat of this bread or drink the chalice of the Lord unworthily, shall be guilty of the body and blood of the Lord. But let a man prove himself, and so let him eat of that bread and drink of the chalice. For he that eateth and drinketh unworthily, eateth and drinketh judgment to himself, *not discerning the body of the Lord.*" If St. Paul understood the words of the institution in the sense of a figure, how could he teach that the unworthy recipients are "guilty of the body and blood of the Lord." How could he condemn the Corinthians for not *discerning* the body of the Lord?

That the words of the institution are expressive of a *real*, and not a *figurative* presence, the adversaries of this doctrine must admit, if they would be consistent, and follow their fundamental rule — namely, to believe what is clearly contained in the Bible, and nothing else. Nothing is more clearly contained in the Bible than the words: "This *is* my body" and "This *is* my blood." Where in the Bible do we find: "This is the figure of my body," or "This is the figure of my blood." This ought to satisfy Protestants.

The unanimous voice of tradition, from the days of the Apostles to our times, tells us, and proves, that the Church of every preceding age understood these words as the Catholic Church of the present time understands them. Could they all have been in error, and the truth have been discovered only by modern *Reformers of the* CHURCH *of Christ—of the work of God?*

CHAPTER XI.

PROOF OF PRESCRIPTION.

THE various and *varying* Churches of the Reformation assert that the Catholic Church did *at first* teach the doctrine of the figurative presence of the body and blood of Jesus Christ in the holy Eucharist, and *afterward changed* it to the doctrine of the Real Presence. That such a change did not take place, is the proposition to be proven in this chapter.

At the time of the Reformation, in the sixteenth century, the Catholic Church, in the East and in the West, taught the doctrine of the Real Presence. Now, from this fact it follows that she always held this doctrine. The first proposition asserts a fact of history; and the Church is willing to abide by the verdict of history on this question of fact.

The second proposition contains the whole force of the argument. From the fact that the entire Catholic Church held the doctrine of the Real Presence in the sixteenth century, we rightfully and validly conclude that she held it at all times since the days of the Apostles. The validity of this inference, which at first hearing, you might feel disposed to controvert, I will establish as follows: Either the Catholic Church always held the doctrine of the Real Presence, or, during the lapse of centuries, a change took place in her teachings on this point. The latter supposition is the assertion of Protestants. They do not, however, prove their assertion. It is their duty to assign the author of the change, the time at which it took place—the circumstances which attended the innovation. They prove none of these important, essential things. There is a rule of logic in accordance with which a gratuitous assertion may, without reasonable offence, be gratuitously denied. Therefore, until the alleged change is proven to have taken place, we *legitimately* conclude that no such change was effected in the doctrine now under consideration.

This little argument would suffice for our purpose, but we cheerfully go still farther, and can readily demonstrate that the aforesaid change was *utterly impossible*, whether we consider the manner in which, or the time at which, it would have been effected.

I. As to the manner.—If a change took place, it must have been either *suddenly* or *gradually*. Now, neither mode is admissible. If you maintain that it took place *suddenly*, you require mankind to believe an astounding miracle, and even an utter *impossibility*. What sane man will believe that simultaneously the Italians, the French, the English, the Spaniard, and the German — the entire Christian Church, in the East and in the West, orthodox and heretical and schismatical — *suddenly* renounced the ancient faith, and began *suddenly* to teach that the Eucharist contained the *true* and *real* and *substantial* body and blood of Jesus Christ? The change could not have taken place *suddenly;* neither could it have taken place *gradually*.

1. Human nature — man's natural disposition — stood in the way — a serious obstacle, when we consider how tenaciously men adhere to the faith of their fathers — how unwilling they are to change it without a sufficient cause.

2. The very nature of the dogma, or article of faith, also precluded the pos-

sibility of the change. The holy Eucharist is not a merely *speculative* dogma, requiring only faith, but a *practical* dogma, which contemplates certain dispositions in the recipient — whether the priest at the altar, or the faithful at the communion-table. Could the whole Catholic world, thus knowing the nature of the holy Eucharist, have allowed the alleged change to be introduced — to be received by all as divine doctrine, coming down from the Apostles, from Christ?

3. But supposing, for argument's sake, that the innovation did take place, would not some vestige of the change remain? Let the assertors of the change assign, at least, the *precise time* at which what they maintain to be *innovation* did not exist. Let them indicate to us a time at which the Real Presence did not exist as a doctrine of the Catholic Church. Let them be so obliging as to furnish the

names of the authors of this doctrinal innovation. The reformers of the sixteenth century were not, and their children of the nineteenth century have not been, able to assign these vestiges, or to prove their existence. History apprises us of almost every great event. It carefully assigns the time, the place, and the circumstances. It faithfully hands down to posterity the names of the good and the great who, in the intellectual or moral order, have proved themselves the benefactors of the human family. With equal fidelity has it made known the names and deeds of other men whose crimes elicit from each succeeding generation universal execration. In like manner does ecclesiastical history inform us of the great events pertaining to the Church. It tells of heresiarchs who attempted to substitute the spurious creations of their fevered brains or proud intellects for the revealed truth of God.

It tells of the nature of the heresy, how it was received, by whom abetted and by whom opposed. It tells, in fine, of all those things, age after age, just as they made their appearance. Such being the case, why do not the reformers take up the history of the Church, and point out to us, and to the world, all the particulars required in proof of their assertion? Why? Because history does not record them. How came history not to contain this record? Was it because the dogma was of less importance than a point of science? Was it less entitled to record than any other fact chronicled? Once more, appealing to honest-minded Christians, I ask, could history have remained silent on a point of such vast importance, had the alleged change ever taken place?

4. Let us for a moment consider the constitution of the Church, and we shall be, if possible, still more convinced that

the doctrinal innovation now in question was impossible. If it had been made by the Pope—the Head of the Church—as some assert, would the various Churches of the East have acquiesced in it? Besides, what man of sane mind can be induced to believe that the entire faithful—the people who receive the doctrine from the pastors, and the pastors teaching—and the bishops "appointed by the Holy Ghost to rule the Church of God," and the Sovereign Pontiff, the successor of St. Peter—could *all* have conspired and agreed to reject the *old* and to receive a *new* doctrine? Could this have been accomplished? Asserting this to be possible, you brand the whole Church—the millions of the faithful, and the tens of thousands of pastors—as so many vile impostors; you make Jesus Himself a lying deceiver, for He promised that the gates of hell should not prevail against His Church; He promised that the Holy Ghost should abide with her, and teach her *all truth;* in one word, you sap the very foundations of Christianity

Thus, whether we consider the Church or her history, or the nature of the dogma, or, in fine, man's own nature, we are forced to admit the impossibility of the change which the reformers assert to have taken place in the doctrine of the Eucharist— the impossibility of either a *sudden* or a *gradual* change.

II. As to the time.—The change was equally impossible in point of time. Permit me to ask my friends of the Reformed Churches, who perseveringly maintain that the Catholic Church *at first* taught the doctrine of the *figurative presence* in the holy Eucharist, and only *subsequently* introduced that of the Real Presence, at what time the change took place? They all, I presume, admit the historical fact, that the Real Presence was the doctrine taught by her in the sixteenth century, and has been her doctrine since that time. Did the change occur between the sixteenth and ninth centuries? It was impossible. The Greek Church was during all that period separated from the Latin or Roman Church. The Greek would not have accepted the novelty in doctrine from the Latin; neither would the Latin have accepted any doctrinal innovation made by the Greek Church. Still, the same doctrine, the Real Presence, is taught in both. How are we to explain the fact? Rival Churches do not enter into a collusion for the purpose of agreeing upon a point of doctrine? The one introducing a change would certainly have found an opponent in the other. The alleged change consequently was not, could not have been, made between the sixteenth and the ninth centuries.

Did it occur between the ninth and the fifth centuries? Again it was impossible, for during that interval of time there were many sects in the East who, in regard to the holy Eucharist, held the same doctrine as the Catholic Church— the Real Presence. In their hostility to her *they* never would have agreed with her to introduce the change in question, and, in her turn, *she* certainly could not have accepted the new doctrine, the innovation, from those sects which she regards as heretics, enemies of the Cross of Christ. Hence, to account for the existence of the doctrine of the Real Presence in all of those sects—Arians, Eutichians, and Nestorians—we must conclude that the doctrine was held in common by them all at the period of their separation. Hence no change was effected in this doctrine of the Church between the ninth and the fifth centuries.

We have thus, at this day, living, speaking witnesses testifying to the important fact that no change has taken place in the doctrine of the Church on the holy Eucharist. How mysterious are the ways of God! Even erring men and foul heresies are made enduring monuments to the immutable truth of God. If the past may be regarded as any criterion of the future, may not the multitudinous *protesting* sects of this day be, for generations yet to come, witnesses, by their very protests, of the faith of the Catholic Church in the various doctrines which they denied.

No change took place in this doctrine of the Church between the sixteenth and the fifth centuries. It was impossible. But may it not have been brought about between the fifth century and the days of the Apostles? Again, I maintain that it was an impossibility. We have still the same obstacles. Besides, we must remember that the Evangelical teachings were, at that early period, too fresh in the minds of the people. A St. John lived beyond the close of the first century. If a change had taken place, or even been attempted, would not the voice of that venerable Apostle — of that illustrious bishop of Ephesus — of that glorious confessor — have denounced the impious innovation? If it had been attempted in the second century, where was St. Ignatius of Antioch — where was St. Polycarp of Smyrna? Were they sleeping sentinels on the watch-towers of the House of the living God? If it had been attempted in the third or fourth century, where were the Irenæuses, the Gregories, the Basils, the Ephrems and the Augustines? Did they all — whose characteristic virtues were zeal, and love of learning, and vigilance — permit the innovation — the criminal change to be made without a word of protest or denunciation? The more reasonable of Protestants have admitted the impossibility of the change at that early period.

Moreover, if the Catholic Church, which

was then, at least, the Church of Christ, changed her doctrine, to what purpose were the promises of her Divine Founder, that she should not err? To what purpose her commission *to teach all nations?* Why did not God Almighty permit the strong arm of pagan Rome to crush her, and the manifold bloody persecutions to blot her out from existence? Why did He allow her to triumph in the midst of her trials, and, after all her struggles, to march onward radiant with victories, and crowned with the laurels with which each succeeding victory graced her brow? Had she been fluctuating, or wavering and changing in faith, why was she not swept from the earth by the all-devastating, barbarian hordes, which, like a deluge, overran the civilized world? If she was so faithless to her trust, oh! why did God protect her — why did the might of His arm sustain her—why did He enable her to challenge our utmost confidence?

The Church, Christian reader, has not *changed* her faith in the holy Eucharist, or *in any other dogma*. She, in every instance, when the immutability of her teaching is assailed, as she now does in regard to the Real Presence, defies the assailant to show *when* the change asserted took place, *how* it was brought about, *by whom* and *where* first broached. Until these questions will have been answered, not by *mere assertions*, but by *unquestionable proofs*, she maintains that her doctrines of to-day have been held and taught in all ages between our times and those of the blessed Apostles. St. Augustine, in a few words, indorses the validity of this mode of reasoning, when he says: "That which the entire Church holds—which owes not its origin to councils, but has at all times been held—is most rightfully considered of apostolic authority."

CHAPTER XII.

CONSECRATION.

OUR faith in the holy Eucharist is clear, well-defined, and unchanging. We believe that Jesus Christ, whole and entire—body, soul, and divinity—is really present on our altar—made present by the mysterious words of Consecration—the same words that Jesus used when instituting this Sacrament and Sacrifice. What He Himself did at the Last Supper, He commanded His Apostles and their successors, the pastors of the flock, to do to the end of time: "Do this for a commemoration of me" (Luke xxii. 19; 1 Cor. xi. 24). This is our faith.

Let it be well understood and well considered, and we shall have no difficulty in seeing the propriety of the various prayers and ceremonies which precede, accompany, and follow the solemn act of Consecration.

Almost immediately before the words of consecration, the following prayer is said: "Which oblation, do Thou, O God, vouchsafe, in all respects, to bless, ✠ approve, ✠ ratify, ✠ and accept, that it may be made for us the ✠ body and ✠ blood of Thy most beloved Son, our Lord Jesus Christ." This prayer, though also only of ecclesiastical prescription, is most solemn, because directly preparatory to the words of Jesus Christ, by which the mystery of the Consecration is effected. The Fathers of the Church of the earliest ages, and ecclesiastical and liturgical writers, in speaking of this prayer, make use of language indicative of the profoundest respect. During it, the priest makes the sign of the Cross three times on the bread and wine in common, and then once on the bread and once on the wine separately. No one can fail to see how appropriately the sign of the Cross is more frequently made as the priest approaches nearer to that awful moment in which the bloody Sacrifice of Calvary is renewed in an unbloody manner in the holy Eucharist. What ceremony could the Church prescribe better calculated to recall to the mind of the officiating minister and of the assisting faithful, the one great and all-sufficient oblation once made on the mount. By the words, "that it may be made for us the body," etc., we are not to imagine that the Church has any doubt as to the omnipotent efficacy of the divine words of consecration. She simply prays that *for us* it may be made the body and blood of the most beloved Son, producing in our regard all those blessed results intended by the God of love who instituted this Sacrament and Sacrifice of love. This prayer continues: "*Who, the day before He suffered, took bread into His holy and venerable hands, and, with His eyes lifted up to heaven, giving thanks to Thee, Almighty God, His Father, He blessed it, brake it, and gave to His disciples, saying, Take and eat ye of this,* FOR THIS IS MY BODY." After pronouncing these words of consecration the priest, kneeling, *adores* and elevates the sacred Host. The faithful, who are supposed to be kneeling at this time, likewise bow down and, with reverential awe, unite in the *adoration*. He then proceeds to the consecration of the chalice, saying: "*In like manner, after He had supped, taking also this excellent chalice into His holy and venerable hands, giving Thee also thanks, He blessed it and gave it to His disciples, saying, Take and drink ye all of this,* FOR THIS

IS THE CHALICE OF MY BLOOD OF THE NEW AND ETERNAL TESTAMENT: THE MYSTERY OF FAITH: WHICH SHALL BE SHED FOR YOU, AND FOR MANY, TO THE REMISSION OF SINS." "*As often as you do these things, you shall do them in remembrance of me.*" Whilst saying these last words, the priest, kneeling, again *adores* and elevates the sacred chalice. The faithful again also *adore*, bowing down as they did during the first elevation. At each time of adoration the clerk rings a little bell to remind the people of the solemn act which is transpiring, and to call them to adoration.

Christian reader, what comment can frail mortals make on the divine words here uttered, and on the stupendous miracle effected by them. The mightiest created intellect is bewildered at the magnitude of the mystery accomplished. The words of consecration carry us back to the days of creation, when the Omnipotent, by His word alone, created light. And God said: "Be light made, and light was made"—"Fiat lux et facta est lux" (Gen. i. 3). It was the same omnipotent "Fiat" that Jesus uttered at the Last Supper, when, taking bread and wine into His blessed hands, He *truly* and *really* changed the substance of the bread into His body, and that of the wine into His blood. It is, at present, the same omnipotent "Fiat" uttered by the priest, as the mouthpiece of Jesus Christ, and in obedience to the divine mandate, which renews the mystery of Transubstantiation. In virtue of the words of consecration pronounced over the bread, the substance of the bread is converted into the body of Jesus. *By concomitance*, where His body is, there His blood and soul also are, as "Christ dieth now no more." Where His body, blood and soul are, there also is His Divinity, for the divine Person of the Son of God having assumed the human nature, never laid it aside, and never will be separated from it. Hence, though only the body of Jesus Christ is spoken of in the words of consecration pronounced upon the bread, still Jesus, whole and entire — blood, soul and Divinity, as well as the body — is really present, and really received by the recipient of the one species of the Eucharistic Sacrament. By the words of consecration pronounced upon the wine, the substance of the wine is converted into the blood of Jesus Christ. Where His blood is *by virtue* of the words of consecration, there also the body and soul and Divinity are *by concomitance*.

Let us, whilst assisting at Holy Mass, bear in mind what a stupendous miracle the Omnipotent God effects at the moment in which the priest pronounces the awful words of consecration. Let us know our faith. Let it be kept vividly before our eyes, and we shall have no difficulty in understanding the various ceremonies and prayers which accompany this solemn act. If, for instance, after the Transubstantiation of the material elements into the body and blood of Jesus Christ, we behold the priest kneeling down most reverently and adoring, then rising and elevating the sacred species, and then we see the entire people devoutly bowed down in heartfelt adoration, we cannot be at a loss to discover the significance of that almost indescribably grand appearance of the interior of a Catholic church at the most solemn moment of the Elevation. It is the moment when the lowly creature, with mind and heart and whole body, pays to the Creator the tribute of adoration. It is the moment when the whole exterior bears testimony to that strong, unwavering, undying faith in the Real Presence, which neither ridicule, nor scoffs, nor persecution, nor death can weaken. It is the moment of time which most resembles the never-ending moment of eternity, in which adoring angels and the just made perfect worship the Deity with "Holy! holy! holy! Lord God of Sabaoth!"

Who has not felt, in the High Mass, how soul-stirring are the loud peals of the church organ — how devotion-inspiring are its sweeter and more soothing strains? But at the moment of the Consecration and Elevation its notes die away gradually, and as the little bell bids the faithful adore, music's sweetest sounds are hushed. All is silent. Solemn, impressive silence! how eloquently dost thou remind us that human words, or the noblest creations of musical genius, are not one half so appropriate for adoration as that solemn, awe-inspiring stillness in which naught is heard, save, perhaps, the throbbings of hearts whose every pulsation is an act of intense divine love.

Endeavor to enter into the spirit of this moment of the Consecration and Elevation. Endeavor to emulate the intensity of angelic fervor, the generosity of seraphic charity. Show to God, to your fellow-Catholics, and also to such as are not of the household of the faith, how strong and vivid your faith is—how powerful and ennobling is its influence upon your exterior. Whilst adoring, you would do well to remember that there are thousands of those for whom, in common with you, Jesus left this mystery of love, who proudly refuse to adore—nay, who impiously ridicule this doctrine, and make it an occasion of blaspheming the God of love.

Remember this not in bitterness, but in pity. Remember it in order to supplicate, in their behalf, that God may lead them to the knowledge and adoption of this holiest and most consoling of revealed truths. Remember it to supply by your fervor and heartfelt devotion for their coldness and indifference and abuses. This is no fanciful idea of the writer's. It was for this last-mentioned purpose that the Latin Church prescribed the Elevation, as we have it now, of the sacred Host, and of the consecrated chalice. It is a historical fact, that this ceremony began in the Western or Latin Church only at the time Berengarius denied the faith in the Real Presence. It was then decreed, in order that the Christian people might thereby be incited to atone for the outrages perpetrated by that heresiarch on the truth of God and on the God of truth Himself. Alas! how many more outrages have we to atone for? How many more heresiarchs have rejected this point of doctrine since the the baneful birthday of the Reformation.

CHAPTER XIII.

REFLECTIONS ON THE CONSECRATION— PRAYERS AFTER THE CONSECRATION.

THE divinely sublime action of the Consecration has been consummated. The priest whose agency the Omnipotent God employed in the accomplishment of the mystery, has himself adored. The faithful too have adored on bended knees, and with heads most reverently bowed down. All this has been done amid that solemn silence so becoming the awe-inspiring, stupendous mystery of the altar.

This is all that human eye beholds at

this august moment; but the eyes of faith penetrate the veil with which Jesus saw fit to hide His really present divine Person, together with His divine and human natures. The eye of faith then beholds that upon which the Eternal Father looks down with complacency— the unbloody, but *real*, renewal of Calvary's great expiatory Sacrifice, and, beholding, beams with joy at the thought and sight of the myriads of priceless graces applied in each Eucharistic Sacrifice to the entire Christian people. Angels too behold more than human vision can discern. Along with poor, frail, but honored mortals, they unite in adoration. If the lovely mystery of Bethlehem elicited from them the song of joy, "Glory to God in the highest, and on earth peace to men of good-will," here and now they may well indulge in similar exultation, for this mystery of Jesus' love truly gives glory to God, and heavenly peace to men. Man has adored; angels have adored. God is honored; man is benefited. Man is lost in admiration of the miracle of power and love displayed at the moment of the Consecration; angels wonder, and, were celestial spirits capable of any thing akin to human passions, would *envy* man's blessed privilege.

Let us now pass to the beautiful and instructive prayers and ceremonies which follow this solemn action. Immediately after the sacred words of consecration, the priest says: "As often as you do these things, ye shall do them in remembrance of me." These words are uttered in accordance with the teaching of St. Paul, who tells the Corinthians that the Eucharistic Sacrament and Sacrifice shall "shew forth the death of the Lord until he come" (1 Cor. xi. 26). They moreover remind the priest of the blessed words of Jesus by which He empowered the legitimately ordained priests of His Church to do what He had done: namely, to change bread and wine into His body and blood: "Do this for a commemoration of me" (Luke xxii. 19).

How many duties to be discharged toward the great God now present upon the altar? How many graces and blessings to be asked for? Conscious how precious these moments are, the priest again, with uplifted hands, betakes himself to prayer, and says: "Wherefore, O Lord, we, Thy servants, as also Thy holy people, calling to mind the blessed Passion of the same Jesus Christ, Thy Son, our Lord; His Resurrection from the dead and admirable Ascension into heaven, offer unto Thy most excellent Majesty of Thy gifts bestowed upon us, a pure ✠ Host, a holy ✠ Host, an unspotted ✠ Host, the holy ✠ bread of eternal life, and the chalice ✠ of everlasting salvation." This prayer is intimately connected with the preceding. "Wherefore" indicates a connection. The priest being commanded to be mindful of the great High Priest, Jesus, in the Eucharistic oblation, obeys the command by affectionately calling to mind the blessed Passion and death really commemorated in the Christian sacrifice; the glorious Resurrection—the model of our spiritual resurrection, and the hope of our rising to immortal life; and His admirable Ascension into heaven, where He "is always living to make intercession for us" (Heb. vii. 25). In union with these great mysteries of the Redeemer's life, the priest offers his sacrifice to the Divine Majesty. What is this offering? A pure Host, to the God of infinite purity. Jesus is that pure Host! A holy Host, to the thrice-holy God. Jesus is that holy Host! An unspotted Host, to the God whose all-seeing eye no spot or stain can escape. Jesus is that unspotted Host! O most holy God, with confidence the most unbounded, we present to Thee our *pure, holy,* and *unspotted* Host—Thy own beloved Son. We offer His sacred body and blood. It is to be remarked that the sign of the Cross made upon the Victim *after* the Consecration has not the same signification as that made *before*. Then that saving sign was made to bless through the mystery of the Cross. We do not, of course, pretend to bless that which is essentially hallowed—the body and blood of Jesus. After the Consecration, it is employed simply to remind the priest and people that it is the Sacrifice of the Cross which is renewed. The five signs of the Cross made at the places indicated are by some liturgists considered reminders of the five sacred wounds of the blessed hands and feet and holy side of the Redeemer.

The next prayer said is: "Upon which vouchsafe to look with a propitious countenance, and to accept them as Thou wast graciously pleased to accept the gifts of Thy just servant Abel, and the sacrifice of our patriarch Abraham, and that which Thy high priest Melchisedech offered to Thee — a holy and unspotted victim." With our clear and well-defined ideas of the Eucharistic Sacrifice, no language employed by the Church in praising the ancient sacrifices can diminish our veneration for that of our altar. We, on the contrary, remember that the best and most laudable of those sacrifices were only figures of the divine reality which we possess. But how can she dignify those oblations which were to be abolished and superseded with the title of *holy Sacrifice* and an *unspotted Victim*? It is simply on account of their relation to our holy and unspotted Sacrifice, of which they were striking figures, and from which they derived all their value and efficacy. The sacrifice offered by Abel was an oblation of the firstlings of his flock—a striking figure of the true Lamb of God one day to be offered. Abel himself is a still more remarkable figure of our blessed Redeemer, put to death by the treachery of a false friend. Abraham's sacrifice was another extraordinary figure of the Sacrifice of the Cross, and of its unbloody renewal upon the altar, forcibly reminding us of the Eternal Father giving His only-begotten Son to be our ransom. The sacrifice of Melchisedech was, perhaps, of all the ancient sacrifices, the one conveying the most vivid image of the Eucharistic Sacrifice—the material elements employed by him being of the same kind as those used by Jesus Christ in instituting the clean oblation now made from the rising of the sun to the going down thereof. Our petition, then, is: O God, Thou who hast been pleased to accept the senseless and inanimate elements, the empty figures offered by those illustrious servants of Thine, how much more wilt Thou look favorably upon and accept our oblation of the sacred body and blood of Thine own consubstantial, co-eternal, and beloved Son.

Then follows another prayer: "We humbly beseech Thee, Almighty God, command these things to be carried, by the hands of Thy holy angel, to Thy altar on high, in the sight of Thy Divine Majesty, that as many as shall partake of the most sacred ✠ body and ✠ blood of Thy Son at this altar may be filled with every heavenly grace and blessing. Through the same Christ our Lord. Amen." The attitude assumed during its utterance is eminently expressive of humility. The priest is reverently bowed down. The more we reflect upon this sacred prayer, the more shall we be filled with religious awe and profound veneration for the august mystery in connection with which it is said. Let us comment briefly upon its most striking expressions: "We humbly beseech Thee, Almighty God." By these few words the Church bids her minister enter into sentiments of that lovely virtue which Jesus commanded us to learn from Himself. No disposition is more appropriate for the priest while Jesus Christ is really present on the altar. How vividly must the thought of the creature standing face to face with the Creator affect him! Though he had retained his baptismal innocence — though he were sinless and pure as the unfallen angels; nay more, though he possessed all the transcendent holiness of the Immaculate Mother of Jesus, he has reason to be *humble* when he remembers the infinite distance between the lowly creature and the most high Creator. Alas! how much greater reason has he to cultivate and cherish humility now, when, perhaps, numberless sins and imperfections painfully remind him of the relation in which he stands to his God — the sin-stained creature in presence of the all-holy God.

The supplication is addressed to the "Almighty God," because the priest's whole mind is filled with the reflection that it is the attribute of Omnipotence which has been so conspicuously displayed in the mystery of transubstantiation. We entreat God to "command these gifts to be carried," etc.; to make use of His absolute and efficacious decree: "He commanded, and all things were created." "By the hands of the holy angel, to Thy altar, on high, in the sight of Thy divine Majesty." Earth is unworthy to retain these gifts — the sacred body and precious blood, soul and divinity of Jesus. The altar on high heaven, the throne of the Lamb alone, is a fitting abiding-place for the

Incarnate God. But who is that angel by whose hands the Victim of the Eucharistic altar is to be carried? Is it that glorious prince of the celestial hosts who, when Lucifer and his associates rebelled, battled with them till they were vanquished and hurled into the abyss? Is it that radiant archangel who was deputed to announce to the incomparable Virgin of Nazareth the glad tidings of the Incarnation so ardently desired by the holy patriarchs, and so distinctly foretold by the prophets? Is it any of those countless myriads of ministering spirits, ever ready to execute the mandates of the Most High? No! Christian reader, the angel here alluded to is, in all probability, the "angel of the testament" (Malacchies iii. 1), and that angel none else but Jesus Himself. Him we beseech to bear His own body and blood, as our Victim, to the throne of the Eternal Father, and there to offer them in our behalf, even as He did once on Calvary's Cross. Oh! with such a Victim offered, and such a mediating Angel offering, have we not reason to hope that they who partake of these gifts will receive the plenitude of heavenly graces and blessings.

Remember, however, that though the Victim is of infinite value, and the great High Priest always "heard for His reverence" (Heb. v. 7), still in vain will the oblation have been made *for us* at the eternal throne, if we bring not to the altar, to this stupendous Sacrifice, hearts truly *contrite and humble.*

CHAPTER XIV.

COMMEMORATION OF THE FAITHFUL DEPARTED.

IN the beginning of the Canon, special prayer was offered for the faithful of the Church militant. Now, while the God of love and mercy is really present on the altar to receive our petitions, that tenderest of Mothers, who forgets none of her children, commands her minister to make fervent supplication for the souls in purgatory. "Death, which dissolves the ties of flesh and blood, respects those of Catholic charity, and seems even to bind them more closely.

The Church believes and teaches, according to the tradition of all time, which is perfectly conformable to Scripture and the light of reason, that beyond this world, between the frightful abyss into which impenitent crime descends forever and the happy abodes open to the souls without stain, there exists a place of temporary suffering, where, according to the words of Jesus Christ, Divine justice demands, even to the last farthing, its dues for faults committed in the journey through life." Besides the doctrine of a purgatorial state, the Church teaches that those therein detained are helped by the prayers of the faithful, and especially by the adorable Eucharistic Sacrifice. How important, then, our duty to our departed friends. Though unwilling to enter into detailed proof of the doctrinal point, I, however, deem it proper to offer some proofs in order to show how unreasonable, how weak, are the objections of those who reject the doctrine in question.

In order to avoid any misunderstanding, let us define the doctrine. Purgatory is a middle state of souls which departed this life free from mortal sin, and yet with some venial faults unatoned for, or some temporal punishment unpaid, or both. This doctrine is denied by the various denominations of our Protestant brethren. Their error, in regard to purgatory, is the logical sequence of the erroneous ideas which they entertain concerning Justification and Satisfaction. They imagine and teach that in the justification of the sinner, along with the guilt of sin (culpa) and the debt of eternal punishment (reatus pœnæ æternæ), all debt of temporal punishment (reatus pœnæ temporalis) is also remitted, so that there remains for the justified no satisfaction to be made. It being in no sense my purpose to treat of Justification and Satisfaction, I content myself with the statement of the error.

Upon what specific grounds is the doctrine of Purgatory denied? Because it is, they say, a novelty introduced by the Catholic Church, and therefore an anti-scriptural teaching. Whilst accusing us of having been guilty of innovation, they, as usual, find it more convenient to content themselves with *mere assertion* than to tell us *when* the doctrinal novelty was introduced, *by whom* abetted and *by whom* opposed. It was taught in the Latin Church, and also in the Greek, in the thirteenth century. This is a fact, and history testifies to the fact. In every age from that period to the apostolic times we find the doctrine clearly taught. (See Bishop England's Works, Vol. I. xxxix. and following Letters, pp. 265–300). If this doctrine was not held during those ages, what mean the prayers for the dead contained in every liturgy of the Western and Eastern Church? Is the teaching anti-scriptural? Do Protestants mean that a doctrine is anti-scriptural when the word, for example, *purgatory* is not found in the Bible? If so, the doctrine of the Trinity is anti-scriptural, because that word, *trinity*, is not contained in the Bible any more than the word *purgatory*. *Consubstantial* expresses an important doctrine in regard to the Son of God. But the word *consubstantial* is not found in the Scriptures. Is the doctrine anti-scriptural for that reason? Those who reject the doctrine of Purgatory, because the word is not found in the Bible, accept and hold the doctrine of the Trinity and of the Consubstantiality of the Son of God, although likewise not found in the Bible. Away with such consistency! In the ordinary affairs of life such conduct would be regarded as ridiculous. Why should it be respected when it is question of the all-important affair of Divine revelation?

Let us adduce a text which the Fathers consider as conveying the doctrine of Purgatory. In St. Matthew xii. 32, we read: "And whosoever shall speak a word against the Son of man, it shall be forgiven him; but he that shall speak against the Holy Ghost, it shall not be forgiven him, neither in this world nor in the world to come." Some sins, then, are forgiven in "the world to come." It cannot be in heaven. Nothing defiled can enter there. It cannot be in hell, for in hell there is no redemption. It must be in a third place. That place the Church calls purgatory. "By no means," exclaim the reformers; "that is not the meaning of the text." And then they resort to ingenuity, and they explain away the words by which they are condemned.

Another text is found, 2 Machabees xii.

46. In verses 43, 44, 45, it is related that the valiant Judas Machabeus sent twelve thousand drachms of silver to Jerusalem, for sacrifice to be offered for the sins of the dead, thinking well and religiously concerning the resurrection. In verse 46 the conclusion is drawn, "It is therefore a holy and wholesome thought to pray for the dead, that they may be loosed from sins." Directly this proves the utility of prayers for the dead, and indirectly it establishes the doctrine of Purgatory. "Oh! no," answer the opponents of this doctrine, "that book does not belong at all to the inspired Scripture." But the Catholic Church, which is the witness of the canonicalness of the books of the Scripture, and *from which* Protestants received the whole Bible, says it is. "But," answer they, "she is mistaken." Well! if the Church has erred in placing this book on the canon of inspired Scriptures, why, may she not

be in error in regard to some others? And if she may have erred in regard to this or any others, then, Protestant brethren, you have no certainty that you possess any inspired writings; and the inspired writings, the Bible, being your *sole* Rule of Faith, your faith is *uncertain*. But faith excludes *uncertainty*. Therefore you have *no real faith*. Ingenuity exercised in rejecting texts of Scripture, or laying aside whole books of the Word of God, leads farther than was expected, and proves a little too much!

I will now proceed to offer two considerations—the first, regarding the reasonableness of the doctrine of Purgatory; the second, the consoling nature of the doctrine of the Church in the matter of prayers for the dead.

I. Whatever we know of the justice and mercy of God, shows the reasonableness of the doctrine of a purgatorial place after death. Men leave this world either extremely wicked—in mortal sin, or perfectly good—free from all sin and all punishment, eternal and temporal, or, in fine, in a sort of middle disposition—not guilty of mortal sin and liable to eternal punishment, but with venial faults unatoned for, and temporal punishment unpaid. The extremely wicked, or the first class, are consigned to everlasting fire. The justice of God demands it. The second class—those free from all sin and all punishment, eternal and temporal—are at once admitted into the abode of bliss—put in possession of those rewards which eye hath not seen, nor ear heard, nor human heart conceived. Now what is to become of the third class, or those called forth from this vale of tears, free indeed from mortal sin, which alone deserves hell, and yet stained with venial fault, or with a debt of temporal punishment unpaid? Will *they* be hurled with the reprobate into the dismal place of eternal weeping and gnashing of teeth? Is mercy to be denied to them? Will no temporary affliction or suffering satisfy the justice of offended Heaven? Will they be received at once into heaven? We teach, the Church teaches, that the all-holy God will not admit them *immediately* into His presence, for "nothing defiled can enter heaven," and that He will not condemn them to the pool of unquenchable fire, but will consign them for a time to a state of suffering wherein the faults even of human frailty shall be atoned for, and the temporal punishment still due paid to the last farthing. Thus the claims of Divine justice and mercy are satisfied.

What is the nature of the punishment which those in purgatory will have to endure? Where is this middle place of punishment? How long will its inmates have to suffer? To what extent are they assisted by our prayers, and, especially, by the adorable Sacrifice? God alone knows. The Catholic Church has decided or defined nothing in regard to these questions. Two things only are defined—of faith, namely, that there is a purgatory, and that the souls therein detained are helped by our prayers and by the holy Sacrifice.

II. I stated that the teaching of the Church in regard to prayers for the dead, whilst useful to them, is to us a most consoling doctrine. The cruel separation caused by death between those whom kindred or friendship bound together is hard enough to bear. See the fond mother in the paroxysms of her grief at the loss of her loved child, or the less demonstrative, but perhaps equally intense sorrowing of the bereaved father. See the orphan child in agonizing distress at the death of a mother, whose sweet words bore joy to the heart—whose smiles of approval so often rendered life's trials tolerable. Tell that grief-stricken mother, that sorrowing father, that agonizing orphan, they may offer fervent prayers and have the holy Sacrifice of the Mass offered to the throne of God, and that that Sacrifice and those prayers will benefit the departed loved ones! Is there not in this praying for our deceased friends something congenial to the noblest impulses of the human heart? Is there not in it something calculated to console and to soothe the aching heart? Tell them, on the contrary, that when their loved ones have ceased to breathe, or been placed beneath the cold earth, they ought not to pray for them—that their supplications are of no avail—that any such communings are impossible between the living and the dead! You tell them that which their nature repels. Should they belong to religious denominations which admit not the lawfulness of prayers for the dead, they turn away with utter disgust from a form of religion which thus does violence to those promptings so natural to the human heart. By the mercy of God, they turn, perhaps, to the holy Catholic Church, which, in virtue of the "Communion of Saints," teaches that the members of the mystical body of Christ are united by the bond of charity, and that those still on earth may commune, by means of prayer, with those in heaven, and those others who, though the friends of God, are not as yet sufficiently pure to be admitted into that blessed abode where naught defiled can enter. They begin to investigate, and, by investigation, are led to discover in the teachings of the Church, *in all other points* as well as in this, that all is conformable and responsive to the reasonable and noble cravings implanted in the human heart by its creator—God.

The priest having arrived at that part of the sacred liturgy wherein he prays for the dead, joining his hands before his breast, says: "Be mindful, O Lord, of Thy servants, N. and N., who are gone before us with the sign of faith, and rest in the sleep of peace." Here he pauses for a moment and prays mentally, and in a special manner, for those having particular claims on his prayers. He then proceeds: "To these, O Lord, and to all that sleep in Christ, grant, we beseech Thee, a place of refreshment, light, and peace. Through the same Christ our Lord. Amen."

A few words of comment on this most consoling and instructive prayer. The minister of the Church is required to pray, first of all, for those who may have special claims to be remembered. Here the faithful ought to address most fervent prayer to the throne of Mercy in behalf of all to whom justice or charity gives a right to special commemoration. Then supplications are made for all that sleep in Christ. Our most solicitous Mother, the Church, tells us what to pray for in behalf of the faithful—" a place of refreshment, light and peace;" of refreshment, in exchange for that of temporary suffering. We know not what manner of suffering they endure. God in His own wisdom, and for reasons worthy of that divine attribute, has seen fit to withhold that knowledge from us. One thing, however, we may safely conclude—namely, that a most important part of their purgatorial suffering consists in the temporary separation from God. Hence we beg of God, our Father and their Father, to accelerate their admission into that abode of bliss where He Himself will be their refreshment and reward exceeding great. We ask for the possession of that place of "light and peace" which can be enjoyed only in that city of God that "hath no need of the sun or moon to shine in it, for the glory of God hath enlightened it, and the Lamb is the light thereof" (Apoc. xxi. 23). It behooves us, then, to enter into the designs and spirit of the Church, and to pour forth our hearts in most fervent prayers for those suffering souls. They are our brethren in Christ Jesus, God being our common Father. Charity impels us to fly to their rescue. Zeal for the glory of God demands this prayer. Each one of those members of the mystical body of Christ, whose time of purification is abridged through the instrumentality of our prayers, becomes a member of that celestial choir whose duty and blessed privilege it is to chant eternally the praises of the Deity. Our own interests also are advanced; for we may rest assured that those whose admission to the fruition of the beatific vision has been hastened by the appeal of the Church militant, will not forget their benefactors on earth, but will become powerful intercessors before the throne of Grace and Mercy.

Pray, then, most fervently for those helpless suffering souls. As often as it may be in your power, have the holy Sacrifice offered in their behalf. Be zealous in your efforts to relieve them; and should it be your lot, one day, to be consigned to the same place of temporary punishment, the mercy of God will raise up fervent souls, who will, in their turn, perform for you the same work of exalted charity.

CHAPTER XV.

NOBIS QUOQUE PECCATORIBUS, ETC., TO THE PATER NOSTER.

FREQUENTLY during these explanations and reflections, we have noticed the Church in her liturgy impressing upon the minds of her minister and of the faithful the importance and necessity of humble and contrite acknowledgment of their sinfulness. Once more, at the end of these solemn prayers intimately connected with the Consecration, she requires her minister at the altar to give utterance to the same salutary sentiments. Immediately after his fervent appeal in behalf of the departed faithful, she puts on his lips the following prayer: "Also to us, sinners, Thy servants, confiding in the multitude of Thy mercies, vouchsafe to grant some part and fellowship with Thy holy Apostles and Martyrs; with John, Stephen, Mathias, Barnabas, Ignatius, Alexander, Marcellinus, Peter, Felicitas, Perpetua, Agatha, Lucia, Agnes, Anastasia, and with all Thy Saints, into whose company we beseech Thee to admit us, not in consideration of our merit, but of Thy own gratuitous pardon. Through Christ our Lord."

The first words of the "Nobis quoque peccatoribus"—"also to us, sinners"—are said in a pitch of voice loud enough to be heard by the faithful. This deviation from that long and impressive silence observed during the preceding part of the Canon, is not without a reason. The Church wishes the entire congregation to unite with the priest in this expression of humility. While saying those first words of the prayer, the priest strikes his breast. This ceremony has always been considered very expressive of those sentiments which the Church at this moment demands. It likens us to the publican, in the Gospel, who was justified for his humility, whilst the proud Pharisee's protestations of justice and righteousness were rejected by God, who always resists the proud. "And the publican," says St. Luke (xviii. 13), "standing afar off, would not so much as lift up his eyes to heaven, but struck his breast, saying, O God, be merciful to me a sinner." We too shall be justified, if our hearts feel what our lips profess, whilst we exclaim, "Also to us sinners." If, whilst we assist at the altar, any feelings of pride arise, let us call to mind the fate of the Pharisee.

What is it that, as sinners, we ask for? Some part and fellowship with the holy

Apostles and blessed Martyrs, in that place of refreshment, light and peace. Then the names of a number of those sainted friends of God are mentioned, in order that we may again avail ourselves of their powerful intercession. The martyrs are named to remind us that if we really desire "part and fellowship" with them in the abodes of bliss, we must imitate, as far as need be, the examples of true Christian heroism which they have left us; we must even, as they did, though not to the same extent perhaps, fight the good fight. If we have been hitherto cowardly in the profession of our faith, with what assurance can we ask for association in heaven with those noble champions and witnesses of the faith. If we have been, and even now are, indifferent, negligent, and cold in obeying God's holy moral law, what presumption to expect the same exceeding great rewards.

The names of holy married women are mentioned to show the faithful that even amid the cares and trials which usually attend the marriage state, God may be served most perfectly. St. Perpetua and St. Felicitas are the models presented. The names of several virgin-martyrs, are given—all eminent for their fervent service of God, but especially for their unconquerable fidelity to the Christian's duty in regard to the angelic virtue of purity. How eloquently do the sufferings and tortures which they endured for the preservation of this lovely virtue condemn Christians of our day. Among those virgin-martyrs, the name of St. Agnes is especially worthy of notice. She suffered for the faith at the tender age of thirteen years. Let youth, who are too apt to palliate their faults by allusions to the weakness consequent on tender years, if they desire " part and fellowship" with those holy servants of God, frequently recall to mind the lovely model of childhood and youth—the glorious St. Agnes. All the saints are then referred to, in order to impress on our minds that what they did—namely, keep the commandments—*we too can do, and must do,* if we desire to be, one day, united with them in the enjoyment of God.

Toward the end of this prayer we acknowledge that our supplication for admission to the company of the blessed, and our hope in that respect, are founded not on any merit of our own, but entirely on that gratuitous pardon which we humbly ask of our most merciful God, through the merits of Jesus Christ our Lord, and especially through the infinite efficacy of the divine Victim offered upon our altar.

At the end of the prayer "Nobis quoque peccatoribus," the priest says: "By whom, O Lord, Thou dost always

✠ create, ✠ sanctify, ✠ vivify, bless and give us all these good things. By Him, and with Him, and in Him, is to Thee, God, the Father Almighty, in the unity of the Holy Ghost, all honor and glory." These concluding words of the second part of the Mass convey some important instructions. We are reminded that to Jesus Christ, the Victim really present on our altar, and to whom we have been pouring forth our most fervent prayer, belongs omnipotent, creative power. "All things were made by him, and without him was made nothing that was made" (John i. 3). It behooves us to notice that it is through Jesus Christ that we are *sanctified*. It is the teaching of St. Paul: "Wherefore, Jesus also, that he might sanctify the people by his own blood, suffered without the gate" (Heb. xiii. 12). His also it is to *vivify* those who by sin, original or actual, are dead to God: "And as in Adam all died, so also in Christ all shall be made alive" (1 Cor. xv. 22), and to bless with most efficacious blessing. He it is that gives us all good things, but especially that greatest and best gift — the Eucharistic Sacrifice and Sacrament. We know these important truths, but it is well to be frequently, daily reminded of them in the holy Mass, in order that we may constantly have recourse to that unfailing, inexhaustible source of every grace and benediction. We are, besides, informed that it is *by* that Mediator, *with* Him, and *in* Him, that we can render true and acceptable honor and glory to the Eternal Father. This is another important, practical lesson, which directs us, whenever we desire to make our thoughts, words and actions tend to the glory of God, to offer them through Jesus Christ, with Him, and in union with His divine actions.

This truly divine and ineffably consoling mystery of the Real Presence, on which we have commented in the second part of the prayers and ceremonies of the Mass, challenge our most devout and reverent attention, our most fervent and heartfelt piety, our intensest and most grateful love. The prayers prescribed for this part of the sacred liturgy are eminently calculated to awaken and nourish the dispositions which the mystery of divine love demands. Were any thing wanting in their impressiveness, the equally instructive ceremonial which accompanies them would supply the deficiency. It is, then, our duty, as Catholics, to bring to the holy altar, and to our august Sacrifice, those perfect dispositions which become the place and the occasion, and to avail ourselves, for the attainment of those dispositions, of the prayers and ceremonies prescribed by the Church in her incomparably grand liturgy.

PART III.

FROM THE PATER NOSTER TO THE END OF THE MASS.

CHAPTER XVI.

PATER NOSTER.

SOLEMN silence, highly befitting the consummation of a mystery of love which no created intellect can fathom, no created tongue adequately express, constituted a striking feature of the portion of the sacred liturgy upon which we have just concluded our considerations. That silence called forth a spirit of holy and inexpressible awe at the power and majesty of the Almighty—a spirit of the most earnest gratitude for the priceless gift of God's boundless love for us—a spirit, in fine, of salutary humility, which awakens in our inmost souls an acknowledgment of our nothingness, and leads us to exclaim with the inspired Psalmist: "What is man that thou art mindful of him, or the son of man that thou visitest him!"

We now pass to the consideration of the third and last part of the Mass—the Communion and Thanksgiving. This portion of the liturgy may also, for greater clearness, be subdivided into three parts —namely, the Preparation for the reception of the holy Eucharist; the Reception itself, or Communion; and the Thanksgiving.

In this work it is question only of that preparation which is made in the Mass,

At the outset we notice the priest raising his voice and saying: "Per omnia sæcula sæculorum,"—"For ever and ever." These are the concluding words of the preceding prayer. Then, with uplifted and outstretched hands, again, in a loud voice, he says: "Oremus,"—"Let us pray." All are invited to unite with him in the prayer which he is about to say in an audible voice. What is this prayer? The Pater Noster—Our Father, or Lord's Prayer—which is prefaced with a few words in which he avers that it is solely in consideration of the divine command, and of the fact that Jesus Christ Himself taught us this form of prayer, that we presume to address God in such terms of filial confidence and childlike familiarity. "Being thus instructed," says the priest, "by Thy saving precepts, and following Thy divine directions, we presume to say: 'Our Father, who art in heaven, hallowed be thy name. Thy kingdom come. Thy will be done on earth, as it is in heaven. Give us this day our daily bread. And forgive us our trespasses, as we forgive them that trespass against us. And lead us not into temptation. But deliver us from evil. Amen.' "

It is hardly necessary to remind you again of the wisdom which characterizes the Church's choice of prayers. We know—from our infancy we have been told—that the Our Father, or Lord's Prayer, is the best of all prayers; the best, because taught by our blessed Redeemer Himself; the best, because it combines simplicity and sublimity—a simplicity which makes it easily understood by the most illiterate—a sublimity which renders it suitable to the most intelligent and spiritual; the best, in fine, because so comprehensive. It is said in a *loud* voice, in the hearing of the entire people, in order that all may unite in it, because it concerns the congrega tion as well as the celebrant to be well prepared for the holy Communion. This is the case even when the faithful do not intend to receive *actually*, for even then they would do well to receive *spiritually* —that is, by an ardent *desire* to be united to Jesus Christ by actual communion. The Lord's Prayer is followed by another in some respects similar to it. "Deliver us, we beseech Thee, O Lord, from all evils, past, present, and to come; and by the intercession of the blessed and everglorious Virgin Mary, Mother of God, and of the holy Apostles, Peter, Paul, and Andrew, and of all Thy saints, mercifully grant peace in our days, that through the assistance of Thy mercy we may be always free from sin, and secure from all disturbance. Through the same Christ, Thy Son, our Lord, who, with Thee and the Holy Ghost, liveth and reigneth, God, world without end. Amen." This prayer is simply a develop ment of the last words of the Our Father. The faithful, through their representative, the clerk, had, by the words, "Deliver us from evil," united with the priest in that prayer. Now he implores deliverance from all evils, past, present, and to come. This favor the Church directs her minister to ask through the intercession of the "blessed and ever-glorious Virgin-Mother of God," because we are taught to believe that the Mother of Jesus has influence with her divine Son, and that she is willing and ever ready to use that influence in behalf of those whose salvation He most ardently desires. The intercession of three of the holy Apostles who shed their blood for the faith, is then also asked. Will their petitions addressed to the throne of Mercy be in vain? In fine, all the blessed are invoked in the same sense—as *intercessors*. As God's faithful and honored servants, we feel that their supplications will be hearkened to, when ours, owing to our sinfulness or imperfect dispositions, would not be entitled to the notice of the all-holy God. But whilst we beg these or any other favors of the peerless Queen of heaven and of the blessed inmates of that abode of bliss, we *never* forget that it is through the merits of Jesus Christ our Lord that all grace is obtained.

During this prayer, the priest having wiped or purified the Patena, or little plate, makes with it the sign of the Cross upon himself. The patena is wiped through respect for the sacred body of Jesus Christ, which is in a moment to repose upon it. By following the ceremonies attentively, we will also observe that the priest kisses the patena. This he does whilst imploring God to grant us *peace*—" mercifully grant us peace in our days"—in order to receive from Jesus that true peace which He brought on earth to men of good-will, and secured for us on the Cross, at the price of His blood. "He is our peace" (Ephesians ii. 14). The peace here prayed for is peace with God, peace with our neighbor, and peace with ourselves—spiritual peace—that peace which is the fruit of justice, and which the wicked man knoweth not: "There is no peace for the wicked, saith the Lord" (Isaias xlviii. 22). He prays for peace as a preparation for the holy Communion, because it is a most indispensable disposition for the worthy and salutary reception of the holy Eucharistic Sacrament — indispensable, because inseparable from that state of grace, justice, and holiness which constitute the first prerequisite of a good Communion. He prays for that peace through the Cross of Christ, because the Cross is the pledge of our true peace—the instrument and mighty weapon by which the Conqueror of the world, the flesh, and the devil, triumphed over these three deadliest foes of true, lasting, and supernatural peace; because, again, that Cross, like the rainbow of old, is, and ever should be, to the Christian, the sign of God's covenant that He wills not the death of the sinner, but that he should live.

Is there not wisdom displayed in the choice of the prayers and ceremonies by which our divinely-guided Mother, the Church, prepares us for the solemn moment of the Communion? And do we not owe a debt of gratitude for the solicitude which she evinces?

CHAPTER XVII.

PAX DOMINI AND AGNUS DEI.

WHILST the priest was saying the last words of the prayer upon which reflections were made in the foregoing chapter, he performed ceremonies worthy of our attention, because full of salutary mystic signification.

Having placed the spotless Host upon the purified patena, kneeling down, he adores the sacred body and blood present upon the altar. This bending of the knee occurs several times between the awful moment of the Consecration and the holy Communion. In every instance, it is expressive of adoration. After the genuflection, the priest takes the sacred Host, and, whilst saying the words, "Through Jesus Christ, our Lord," etc., breaks it over the chalice, and then makes the sign of the Cross three times with the particle of the Host, saying aloud: "Pax ✠ Domini sit ✠ semper vobis ✠ cum"—"May the peace of our Lord be always with you." To these words the clerk answers: "Et cum spiritu tuo"—"And with Thy spirit." Then one part of the Host is put into the consecrated chalice, and the following prayer is said. "May this mixture and consecration of the body and blood of our Lord Jesus Christ be to us that receive it effectual to eternal life. Amen." It is to be noticed that in taking the sacred Host, it is only with the thumb and forefinger, or index, that the priest touches the consecrated species. Indeed, in his ordination, those fingers are especially anointed with holy oil, and sanctified for the touching of the sacred body and blood of Jesus Christ. There is a rubrical prescription requiring him not to touch any thing else with those fingers from the moment of the Consecration until they have been washed after the Communion. Hence those fingers are kept joined together, except when the sacred species are touched. Why is the Host broken? In conformity with what Jesus did when taking bread; He blessed, *broke*, and gave to His disciples, and said: "Take ye and eat. This is my body" (Matt. xxvi. 26). Why is one part put in the consecrated chalice? The separate consecration of the element of bread by which its *substance* is converted into the body of Jesus Christ, and of the element of wine by which its *substance* is made the blood of Christ, represented the separation of the body and blood of Jesus, which took place in his death. Now the blending or commingling of the two species signifies the reunion of that body and blood and soul in His resurrection. Whilst thus commemorating those two great mysteries of our blessed religion, we should resolve to profit by them. By this means only will the expressive ceremonial here considered contribute to the realization of the Church's wish: "May this mixture and consecration of the body and blood of our Lord Jesus Christ be to us that receive it effectual to eternal life." The death of Jesus was the ransom paid for our sins, "who was delivered for our sins" (Romans iv. 25), and His resurrection is the means of our justification: "and rose again for our justification" (Romans iv. 25). How salutary would not reflection on those two great truths, as often as we assist at the holy Mass, prove.

The next prayer is the Agnus Dei. The priest, after having again bended the knee and adored Jesus really present on the altar, bowed down in the attitude of profound reverence, says thrice: "Agnus Dei, qui tollis peccata mundi, miserere nobis"— "Lamb of God, who takest away the sins of the world, have mercy on us." At the end of the third Agnus Dei, the priest says: "Dona nobis pacem"— "Give us peace"— instead of "Miserere nobis" or "Have mercy on us." Every circumstance in this ceremonial is worthy of our attention. The bending of the knee express *faith* and *adoration*. The bowing down is a most appropriate attitude for penitents, and is expressive of *humility*. The sentiment of humility is itself peculiarly becoming, at a moment when we are preparing for the most sublime and intimate union with Jesus Christ—a union by which we are exalted to a position so incomprehensibly high, that the mightiest created intelligence could never have conceived its possibility. *Then* humility is becoming, for "he that humbleth himself shall be exalted." "The Lamb of God," etc., is said *thrice*, to signify the earnestness of our petition and our holy importunity. Each time he strikes his breast, to express compunction and contrition of heart. By humility we acknowledge our sinfulness. That acknowledgment should be accompanied with sorrow, contrition: "A *contrite* and *humble* heart, O God, thou wilt not despise" (Ps. l. 19). In requiem Masses, instead of the "Have mercy on us" and "Give us peace," the celebrant says: "Give them rest," "Give them rest," and "Give them eternal rest."

The prayers which follow the Agnus Dei convey very useful instructions. Those prayers are: "Lord Jesus Christ, who saidst to Thy Apostles, I leave you my peace, I give you my peace, regard not my sins, but the faith of Thy Church, and grant her that peace and unity which are agreeable to Thy will; who livest and reignest for ever and ever. Amen."

This first prayer is not said in Masses for the dead.

"Lord Jesus Christ, Son of the living God, who, according to the will of Thy Father, hast, by Thy death, through the co-operation of the Holy Ghost, given life to the world, deliver me by Thy most sacred body and blood from all my iniquities and from all evils, and make me always adhere to Thy commandments, and never suffer me to be separated from Thee: who, with the same God the Father and the Holy Ghost, livest God for ever and ever. Amen."

"Let not the participation of Thy body, O Lord Jesus Christ, which I, though unworthy, presume to receive, turn to my judgment and condemnation, but through Thy mercy may it be a safeguard and remedy both to soul and body; who, with God the Father, in the unity of the Holy Ghost, livest and reignest for ever and ever. Amen."

Upon these most excellent prayers a few reflections are proper. The truly fervent children of the Church, animated by a lively faith, firm hope, and ardent charity, will make a host of others which brevity here precludes. The mercy and peace of God having been implored through the Lamb of God who taketh away the sins of the world, two things, in particular, are prayed for in the first of these three prayers—the *peace* of God and that *unity* which is agreeable to the Divine will. That peace is asked of Jesus in virtue of His own promise: "Peace I leave you; my peace I give you" (John xiv. 27). This seems to have been the Redeemer's favorite salutation to His beloved disciples. The reader of the Epistles of the great Apostle of the Gentiles must also have noticed that this peace is his frequent and most earnest salutation and wish in behalf of those whom his zeal and labors introduced into the Christian family. This blessed peace must, then, have been of great importance. The world, too, has its peace to offer. The Prince of the world has for worldlings a salutation of peace. But the peace offered by the world is unreal and delusive, as all its votaries have experienced. Solomon, the renowned monarch of the Jewish people, sought peace in worldly honors, in worldly riches, and in worldly pleasures. No one, in all probability, made a fairer experiment of what manner of peace this world can give. His decision is a lesson for us: "Vanity of vanities, and all is vanity" (Ecclesiastes i. 2). St. Augustine, previously to his conversion, essayed that peace which wordly pleasures pretend to impart, and his testimony deserves to be written in letters of gold: "For

Thyself, O God, hast Thou made us, and our hearts cannot rest till they rest in Thee." Well, then, may we supplicate the hidden God of our altar for that supernatural peace — that essential disposition for the worthy reception of the holy Communion.

In the same prayer we ask for that "unity which is agreeable to the Divine will"—a unity of faith, which excludes all heresies, schisms, and unbecoming wranglings from the Church of the living God—a unity of charity, by which all the children of the Church of our day may, like the first Christians, have but "one heart and one soul" (Acts iv. 32).

In the second prayer, commemorating the action of the eternal Father and of the co-eternal holy Spirit in the work of man's redemption, we implore other great blessings of Jesus, the second adorable Person of the living, triune God. We ask these blessings through the mystery of love being commemorated on the altar. What are these other blessings? First, deliverance from "all our iniquities and from all evils." If these our miseries are viewed with the eye of faith, with what earnestness will we not appeal to Him who is able and willing to aid us— the Son of God. Secondly, that He would always make us adhere to His commandments—that He would, each time that we assemble around the altar, impress deeply upon our minds that the burden of His commandments is light, and the yoke of His holy law sweet. Thirdly, that He will never suffer us to be separated from Himself—that He will enable us to see most vividly, and always to bear in mind, that as the branch cannot bear fruit of itself unless it abide in the vine, so neither can we unless we abide in Him (John xiv. 4). But if we pray most fervently and most properly for union with Jesus Christ in time during this life, oh! how much more reason have we to beseech Him in accents of the most heartfelt prayer, that it may never be our wretched lot to be separated from Him during eternity.

In the third prayer there is more special allusion to the holy Communion, for which preparation is being made. The thought and the consciousness of his unworthiness rush upon the priest. He begs the Lord Jesus to make allowance for that unworthiness. A sense of holy fear seizes upon him! The solemn warning of St. Paul is vividly before his eyes: "Therefore, whosoever shall eat of this bread or drink the chalice of the Lord unworthily, shall be guilty of the body and blood of the Lord. But let a man prove himself, and so let him eat of that bread and drink of the chalice. For he that eateth and drinketh unworthily, eateth and drinketh judgment to himself, not discerning the body of the Lord"

(1 Cor. xi. 27, 28, 29). With fear and trembling he implores that such may not be his fate, but that the holy Communion may be for him "a safeguard and remedy both to soul and body"—the pledge of everlasting life and of a glorious resurrection: "He that eateth my flesh and drinketh my blood hath everlasting life, and I will raise him up in the last day" (John vi. 55).

Such are a few of the edifying reflections suggested to the priest and faithful by the prayers and ceremonies of this portion of the Mass. Let us enter into the spirit of the Church, or rather of the Holy Ghost, who guides and inspires her in all things pertaining to the sanctification of the children of God. Thus shall we most effectually prepare ourselves for the reception of the holy Communion.

CHAPTER XVIII.

THE PRIEST'S COMMUNION.

IN the preceding chapter, when reflecting upon the prayers uttered in preparation for the holy Communion, we beheld a holy fear and sentiments of confidence contending alternately for the mastery over the priest.

Confidence triumphs. Kneeling down, he adores the Incarnate God really present on the altar. Rising, with all that confidence which the invitation of Jesus warrants, he takes the sacred Host, and says: "I will take the bread of heaven, and call upon the name of the Lord."

He trembles at the thought of his unworthiness, but adverts to the threat which love for man prompted the God of love to make: "Amen, amen, I say to you, except you eat the flesh of the Son of man, and drink his blood, you shall not have life in you" (John vi. 54). He also remembers the consoling assurances of the same loving Redeemer: "He that eateth my flesh and drinketh my blood, abideth in me, and I in him." "As the living Father hath sent me, and I live by the Father; so he that eateth me, the same also shall live by me." "He that eateth this bread, shall live forever" (verses 57, 58, 59). With these or similar confidence-inspiring reflections, holding the consecrated Host, he bows down in the attitude of profound reverence, and says: "Lord, I am not worthy that Thou shouldst enter under my roof; say but the word, and my soul shall be healed." This little prayer, with the attitude in which it is uttered, is solemnly impressive. The moment has arrived in which he is to receive Jesus, true God and true man, under the sacramental forms. Though he has endeavored to approach the altar with purity of heart and soul; though the mandates of a loving and loved Redeemer inspire confidence; though he has, from the Confiteor, at the beginning of the Mass, to the present moment entertained and expressed sentiments of humility like those of the poor publican, still a salutary fear, a holy and befitting awe, prompted by a lively faith, causes him to exclaim: "Lord, I am not worthy that Thou shouldst enter under my roof; say but the word, and my soul shall be healed." These words, with a little alteration, taken from the sacred Word of God, are beautifully appropriate, and admirably calculated to awaken sentiments proper for the moment of the holy Communion.

They were first uttered by the centurion on an occasion infinitely less solemn. Need I remind you how much our Saviour was moved by this simple, heartfelt expression of the centurion's faith? Need I remind you that this fervent expression was immediately followed by the recompense due to faith? This short prayer elicited from the God of truth that remarkable exclamation: "Amen, I say to you, I have not found so great faith in Israel" (Matt. viii. 10). Whilst, therefore, the success that attended the centurion's fervid appeal inspires confidence, have we not too many reasons to fear that the lukewarmness of our faith, contrasted with the lively and persevering faith of the centurion, should draw down upon us the withering, but most just rebuke administered by our divine Redeemer to His chosen people: "Amen, I say to you, I have not found so great faith in Israel." Amen, I say to you,

I have not found so great faith in my chosen Christian people.

Apart from the reflections suggested by the words now commented upon, what a host of others, equally salutary and becoming this solemn moment, present themselves to the minds of the faithful. "On whatsoever side I cast my eyes, I behold nothing but proofs of my unworthiness. If I turn them inward, what multiplied prevarications. How many weaknesses fostered and indulged. How many inspirations neglected—how many duties unfulfilled. How many irregular thoughts and inordinate desires—how many faults unwept, unexpiated, unrepented! Will the thought of what I am and what Thou art inspire confidence? Can it be *God* that I am about to receive? Yes, my faith tells me so, and with most unfaltering belief I assent. I am to receive Him whom the immensity of the heavens is too bounded to contain;

Him whose footstool this vast and magnificent universe is. However vast and inexpressibly grand the splendor of that court formed by the myriads of radiant spirits that surround His throne, it is infinitely disproportionate to His supreme Majesty; however deep, and solemn, and majestic the canticles chanted by this countless multitude of saints and angels, it is infinitely short of what is due Him." Overwhelmed with these awe-inspiring considerations, what motive of confidence can I find to encourage my poor soul? Prostrate at the foot of the holy altar, I will exclaim: Here, O Lord, Thou art a hidden God; Thou hast, in mercy and love, concealed the overpowering grandeurs of Thy divinity. Still, beholding Thee even through this veil, I am again forced to exclaim: "Lord, I am not worthy that Thou shouldst enter under my roof; say but the word, and my soul shall be healed." One word, O Lord! Say that one word, and my poor soul shall be healed of all her maladies. Thy omnipotent word sufficed to create — to cure the blind, the lame, and the afflicted of every kind. Thy word sufficed to restore the dead to life, and, more than all, to institute the adorable Eucharistic Sacrament and Sacrifice.

Having by prayer, and humility, and sorrow of heart prepared for the reception of Thy sacred body and blood, he proceeds with childlike confidence to partake of the heavenly banquet to which Divine love invites him. The moment of the holy Communion has arrived. Elevating the sacred Host and making the sign of the Cross with it, he says: "May the body of our Lord Jesus Christ preserve my soul to life everlasting. Amen." Then bowing down with all that reverence and devotion which so divinely solemn a moment demands, he receives the consecrated Host. He rises immediately, and, with his hands devoutly joined, spends a few moments in silent adoration. The prayer, "May the body of our Lord Jesus Christ preserve my soul to life everlasting. Amen," is not to be understood as expressing any doubt in the mind of the priest as to the efficacy of the sacred body of Jesus to produce the blessed results promised by Him, "If any man eat of this bread, he shall live forever" (John vi. 52), but rather that in his case there may be no obstacle in his heart to the Divine food which he is on the point of receiving. The *silent* adoration is also very instructive. The priest, fully conscious that no human mind can comprehend the Eucharistic mystery, or human tongue do justice to its greatness, prefers to remain in a silence more eloquent than words, and to let the heart with its own more prayerful language discharge the duty of adoration. Ah! if mortal eyes could see what transpires in the heart of the fervent, well-prepared recipient of the holy Communion—that ineffable union between the creature and the Creator—that sweet, indescribable communing going on during that silent adoration—that lavish profusion of God's choicest graces—that enrichment of the poor sojourner in this land of exile—that astounding abasement of the Almighty, Eternal God, and deification of lowly man! This privilege is denied, for reasons worthy of Divine wisdom.

After the few moments of silent adoration, the priest says: "What return shall I make to the Lord for all He has given me." He then makes another genuflection preparatory to receiving the precious blood. With the patena he carefully gathers up whatever particles of the sacred Host may have remained on the corporal, and puts them into the consecrated chalice. Then taking the chalice, he says: "I will take the chalice of salvation and call upon the name of the Lord. Praising, I will call upon the Lord, and shall be saved from my enemies." Immediately afterward, raising the chalice and making the sign of the Cross with it, he says: "May the blood of our Lord Jesus Christ preserve my soul to life everlasting. Amen." The prayers and ceremonies here are much the same as those already spoken of in connection with the receiving of the sacred Host, and suggest like reflections, even as the act demands like sentiments of devotion, reverence, and adoration. Hence here again the priest pauses a little in silent prayer.

The Communion is deemed essential to the integrity of the Sacrifice. Hence, notwithstanding the strict law requiring the receiver of the Holy Eucharist to be fasting, the Church allows another priest, even *not fasting*, to consume the consecrated species in the event of the celebrant being unable to do so, owing to sickness, sudden death, or any other cause.

To what a multitude of perfect dispositions do not the prayers and ceremonies here prescribed give rise? Here, again, is the Church, in virtue of her admirable ceremonial legislation, entitled to our profoundest gratitude.

CHAPTER XIX.

THE COMMUNION OF THE LAITY.

IMMEDIATELY after the priest's Communion, that of the faithful takes place. Whilst the celebrant was saying the prayer, "Domine non sum dignus," etc.—"Lord, I am not worthy," etc., a few strokes of the little bell reminded them that the blessed moment of the holy Communion was at hand. What are the prayers and ceremonies which accompany the Communion of the faithful? The clerk, in the name of those who are to partake of the heavenly banquet, says the Confiteor, or formula of general confession, in order that they may renew and express publicly those sentiments of contrition and humility so proper for the reception of the Eucharistic Sacrament. At the end of the Confiteor, the priest, having taken the ciborium, which contains the most blessed Sacrament, out of the tabernacle and uncovered it, kneels and adores. Then, turning toward the faithful, he pronounces the general absolution: "May Almighty God be merciful unto you, and, forgiving you your sins, bring you to life everlasting." The clerk answers: "Amen." "May the Almighty and merciful Lord grant you pardon, absolution, and remission of your sins." The clerk again says: "Amen." At this prayer the priest makes the sign of the Cross over those who are about to receive the holy Communion, to remind them that all pardon and absolution is through the mystery of the Cross.

Having turned to the altar, he takes

the ciborium in his left hand and one of the sacred Hosts in his right, and, facing the people, with the Host slightly elevated, says: " Ecce Agnus Dei, ecce qui tollit peccata mundi"—" Behold the Lamb of God, behold Him, who taketh away the sins of the world." This consoling and confidence-inspiring prayer is immediately followed by the same beautiful words which the priest said in preparation for his own Communion: " Domine, non sum dignus," etc.—" Lord, I am not worthy that Thou shouldst enter under my roof; say but the word, and my soul shall be healed." This prayer is said thrice.

All the prayers and ceremonies of this part of the Mass will, if seriously reflected upon, contribute not a little to stir up in the hearts of the Christian people those sentiments which become the moment and the act of Communion. When the priest, bending the knee, *adores*, are not those kneeling at the holy table forcibly invited to enter into that essential disposition—adoration? When he, as the minister of the Most High, implores for those who are to be refreshed and nourished with the body and blood of the incarnate, all-holy God, pardon and full remission of their sins, are not they themselves eloquently reminded that it behooves them to unite, in all fervor, in that most important supplication? When the priest, elevating the sacred and adorable Host, bids them behold the Lamb of God beneath the sacramental veils—beneath the form and appearance of bread, and bids them behold Him as the merciful Lamb that taketh away the sins of the world, do not the faithful, bowing down, make a strong and public act of faith in the mystery presented for their credence? Should they not experience within themselves an intense longing to be united to the loving Redeemer? When the "Domine, non sum dignus," etc.—"Lord, I am not worthy," etc., is said by the celebrant in the hearing of the people and for their benefit, will it not awaken, in those who are, ere long, to receive the hidden God, the same salutary sentiments—fear and trembling, and holy, childlike confidence—which it elicited from the priest himself when he uttered this prayer in preparation for his holy Communion?

Having concluded these prayers and ceremonies, he proceeds at once to the giving of the holy Sacrament. In administering the holy Eucharist, he says: "May the body of our Lord Jesus Christ preserve thy soul to life everlasting. Amen." This prayer is repeated in behalf of each person to whom the holy Sacrament is given. In the primitive Church the priest used to say: "This is the body of our Lord Jesus Christ." The one receiving answered: "Amen." The same expression of cordial assent, of faith, may, with advantage, be employed whilst the priest says: "May the body of our Lord Jesus Christ preserve thy soul to life everlasting."

At this point, several important questions present themselves. How should the faithful receive holy Communion? What disposition should they bring to this most holy action? Why do the laity, and those in clerical orders, and *even* priests when not offering the adorable Sacrifice, receive the sacrament of the Eucharist under the form of bread alone, and not under the forms of bread and wine? The first and second of these questions I propose to answer here. The third will be treated in the following chapter.

I. How should the faithful receive the holy Communion? When should they come to the altar railing or holy table? Just at the signal given by the ringing of the little bell, at the " Domine non sum dignus"— before the priest's Communion. What should they do on their arrival at the railing? Kneeling down reverently, they should hold the Communion-cloth in such manner that if the sacred Host, or any particle of it, happened to fall from the priest's hand, it would fall on the cloth, and not on the floor. They should, whilst waiting their turn to receive, keep the head most reverently bowed down. When on the point of receiving, the head should be held *erect* and the eyes be modestly cast down. When the priest is about to give the sacred Host, the mouth ought to be kept moderately opened, and the tongue extended a little, in order that he may have no difficulty in placing the Host upon the tongue. This point is of importance, as many hold the head so bowed down at the moment of Communion, that the priest experiences difficulty in giving the sacred Host. Others, failing to open the mouth or extend the tongue a little, occasion the priest a great deal of uneasiness lest he should drop the blessed Sacrament. When the sacred Host has been placed upon the tongue, the communicant should *quietly* draw back the tongue and close the lips. When the holy species have become a little moistened, they should be immediately swallowed with reverence. Should the Host, or any part of it adhere to the palate, let it be loosened with the tongue, but *by no means* touched with the fingers. Great care must be taken to avoid spitting for some time—eight or ten minutes—after receiving, lest any particle of the Host might still remain in the mouth. By attending to these directions, this holy and most august action will be performed becomingly, and most, if not all, of that awkwardness so out of place at the holy table will be avoided.

II. What dispositions should be brought to the reception of the holy Eucharist? A great purity of heart and soul — exemption from all grievous or mortal sins. This is the first disposition, so essential that without it the reception of the holy Sacrament would be a frightful sacrilege. After that state has been lost by mortal sin, that essential purity can be regained only by a good confession. The recipient of the body and blood of Jesus ought also to be free as possible from attachment to venial sin.

These dispositions are, however, by no means sufficient. They consist merely in removing from our hearts whatever could displease the eye of our most distinguished, divine Visitor. The heart and soul must be adorned. What are the ornaments which the Christian should introduce into his heart and soul on this occasion? All thanks to God, they are ornaments within the reach as well of the poorest beggar as of the wealthiest prince—Christian virtues. Faith is the first of these soul-ornaments, most pleasing in the eyes of God, since by it the Christian bows down in most reasonable assent to all revealed truths, but especially, in the holy Communion, to the great and incomprehensible mystery of the Eucharist. Faith will pour a flood of light upon the mystery of love. It will impart to the Christian eye a *supernatural* quickness of perception and keenness of vision by which much of the length and breadth and depth of the grandeurs contained in this mightiest work of Divine love will be seen, even through those veils which now hide from human gaze the sweet, consoling, grand realities of the Eucharistic mystery.

The Divine virtue of Hope is another ornament peculiarly becoming as a preparation for the reception of this great sacrament. Have we not every reason to confide in that goodness which, despite our unworthiness, gives us the greatest gift in the power of God to confer. Hope —the bright angel of man's journey through this vale of tears—will stand by, telling the recipient of the Eucharistic Sacrament that all is well, to fear not. Hope condemns presumption, banishes despair. With a joy-beaming countenance this radiant angel points to the confidence-inspiring mystery of the sacred body and blood, and, with an expression calculated to cheer up the most despondent, sweetly asks: Will the God who in mercy and love gives His own well-beloved Son to you, refuse aught of grace and blessing?

But the divine virtue of Charity is the richest ornament with which the Christian soul can be adorned for the reception and entertainment of her distinguished Visitor and Guest-the incarnate God. It renders her more beautiful and brilliant, more lovely and acceptable to God, than aught else can. The measure of His delight, with His sacramental visit to the soul, will be proportionate to the degree and perfection of this matchless virtue. If our Saviour, for whose visit we prepare, loved us first, and loved us with the utmost love of which even God was capable, have we not the most cogent reasons to love Him—to return the *mite* of our intensest and most perfect love for His astounding, infinite love? Bring to the reception of the Sacrament of Divine love a most perfect love, and then the heart and soul will be a tabernacle richer and more acceptable than any material one, though its floor and walls and ceiling were of the purest gold. Charity—a participation of that Divine fire which is kept alive in the abodes of bliss by the face-to-face vision and blessed fruition of the all-holy God—will, in the holy Com munion, in the sacramental possession of the same God, inflame the Christian heart and soul with all that intense fervor which our holy religion's less perfect union of man with God demands. Then will coldness and tepidity, which are now, alas! too often brought to the holy altar, be forever banished. Then will we be entering into the designs of our Redeemer Himself: "I am come to send fire on the earth, and what will I but that it be kindled" (Luke xii. 49).

Introduce Humility too. It will impart a new lustre to every Christian virtue. Nay, more, it is the foundation of all virtues, and without it they cannot exist. It is their very soul and vital principle. Without it they are lifeless and unreal. Gather together as many other virtues as possible. They are like so many gems which impart a brilliancy well nigh celestial to that abiding-place which love prompted the divine Institutor of the Eucharistic Sacrament to select in the hearts and souls of men.

Oh! were Faith and Hope and Charity and Humility more faithfully and fervently cultivated by the recipients of the adorable Sacrament of our holy altar, our tender Mother, the holy Church, would not have to weep, as she now does over the innumerable fruitless communions; the faithful would no longer be tortured with those well-grounded apprehensions which the unprofitable reception, for years, of the sacred body and blood awakens.

Before concluding this chapter, I ought perhaps, to mention the disposition of the body which are also required. The Church, through respect for the holy Eucharist, has ordained that those receiving Communion be *fasting from the midnight before*, except when the Sacrament is received in danger of death, as a Viaticum. This fast is of the strictest kind, forbidding eating or drinking of any thing whatsoever. To receive the holy Communion when conscious of having broken this fast, is a mortal sin, being *a violation of an important law*. The whole exterior of those who approach the holy table should be modest and respectful. That modesty and respect, the necessity of which all must unhesitatingly admit, are, I regret, too frequently not sufficiently visible. There should be nothing in the *dress, gait,* or *countenance,* to which modesty, respect, and reverence, could object; and there will not be, if the interior dispositions already referred to exist in the heart and soul.

CHAPTER XX.

EFFECTS OF A WORTHY COMMUNION—COMMUNION UNDER ONE FORM.

I SHALL in this chapter offer a few reflections on the effects of a worthy Communion, and answer the doctrinal question: "Why do the laity, and even the clergy, when not offering the Sacrifice, receive this Sacrament under the form of bread only, and not under the form of bread and wine?"

If I attempt to point out some of the admirable and consoling effects of the worthy Communion, far be it from me to imagine that mortals can convey any adequate ideas of so mysterious a subject. The Catechism directs our attention to five of the principal effects of Communion.

I. Communion unites us intimately with Jesus Christ, who becomes really our spiritual nourishment. This intimate union is, in reality, the most glorious effect of this Sacrament. The happiness of heaven consists in a most admirable union of the blessed with God. By it they possess Him, they see Him "face to face," they enjoy Him! The worthy communicant is most mysteriously united to God, to Jesus Christ, the second adorable Person of the triune God; he possesses God, he enjoys God. The great difference between the sacramental union and the union of the beatific vision is, that in the latter God is seen "face to face," perfectly, whilst in the former He is seen only imperfectly, with the eye of faith and through the veil which eternal Wisdom has seen fit to interpose between us and the Divine realities of the holy Sacrament. Notwithstanding this difference, the more we reflect on the admirable union effected by the holy Communion between the Christian soul and her God, the more do we perceive in it of a marvellous approach to that ineffable union which exists in the abodes of bliss. Our Divine Redeemer Himself has lovingly condescended to point out to us some of the features of this blessed union which, as it were, converts this land of exile and vale of tears into a real heaven. He tells us that He is the living Bread which came down from heaven; that if any man eat of this bread he shall live forever. Then He tells what that bread is: "And the bread that I will give is my flesh, for the life of the world." "My flesh is meat indeed, and my blood is drink indeed." "He that eateth my flesh and drinketh my blood, *abideth in me, and I in him.*" Are not our food and drink most intimately united to us? Physiologists have expatiated on this question, and their explanations of the manner and extent of the conversion of our nourishment into the constituents of the human body, satisfy us that a marvellous union takes place. Now, in the spiritual and supernatural order, the body and blood of Jesus—the true bread from heaven, that bread which is His flesh—will also prove a nourishment, the nourishment of the soul. And so intimately will this Divine nourishment become united to the soul, that Jesus, the very God of truth, did not hesitate to say: " He that eateth my flesh and drinketh my blood, *abideth in me, and I in him.*"

Angels, Christian reader, favored by the omnipotent God with a vision of what transpires on the occasion of the holy Communion, are lost in amazement at the nature of the union effected between God and man in the Eucharistic Sacrament. With all that intensity of fervor which characterizes angelic worship, they praise and thank Him who sitteth at the right hand of the Eternal Father for this matchless institution of Divine love. But oh! it is sad indeed to behold Christian man, for whom alone the Redeemer's greatest love established this mysterious means of almost heavenly union with God, so indifferent, so negligent, so cold. This indifference points to want of *lively* faith. This neglect establishes beyond question an alarming fact—that the fires of Divine love are well nigh extinguished.

Recipients of this noblest of all Divine institutions, awake from your spiritual lethargy to a *sense of duty* and to a *sense of danger!* Resolve, by the aid of grace, henceforth to bring to the reception of the holy Eucharist, to the Communion, that perfection of dispositions which is indispensable for union with God. Then, and not till then, need you expect to realize the blessings implied in the intimate and mysterious union which is the first and most consoling effect of the holy Communion. Then, and not till then, will you appreciate the important teaching of the ascetical writers that *one* Communion ought to make you saints. Then, and not till then, will you begin to taste those sweet, celestial delights which fervent communicants have experienced.

II. The holy Communion *increases* in us the spiritual life of grace. Notice the word *increases*. As has been already stated, the first prerequisite for a good Communion is the state of grace. The soul then is supposed to be in possession of grace—its spiritual life. The holy Communion *increases* this life of grace. The soul endowed with the life of grace is pleasing in the eye even of the thrice-holy God. It is lovely and beautiful and radiant beyond any thing that human imagination can fancy. Its loveliness, beauty, and radiancy are thus transcendent simply because they are participations of the infinite loveliness, beauty, and radiancy of God Himself. If the soul in the first stages of this spiritual life of grace possesses the qualities here predicated of it, who can form any adequate idea of the additional degrees of these qualities communicated by the sacramental union of the incarnate Son of God, with that holy soul?

Let it be impressed upon the mind so deeply as never to be effaced, never forgotten—that the degree of increase of this spiritual life of grace will be proportionate to the degree of perfection of dispositions brought to the reception of the holy Sacrament. Let communicants also bear in mind that the glory of God as well as their own interests, demands that every effort be made to render each holy Communion productive of the greatest possible *increase* of the spiritual life of grace.

III. The holy Communion moderates the violence of our passions, and weakens concupiscence. What Christian is ignorant of the existence of those passions? Who has not, more or less frequently experienced their violence? At times, it is *one* of those domestic foes that assails the child of God; at others, it is a *multitude* that unite and advance, as it were, in solid column, and battle so *fiercely* and so *violently* for the ruin of the immortal soul, that by no human means can the Christian combatant triumph? To what means is he to recur? He must fly to God, on the wings of prayer the most fervent. This is the most general means placed by the mercy of God at man's disposal. It is always possible, nay easy, with lips and heart, to invoke the All-powerful. There is every inducement to do so. The Eternal Father's well-beloved Son says: "Amen, amen, I say to you, if you ask the Father any thing in my name, he will give it you" (John xvi. 23). Who does not see that if simple, heartfelt, earnest invocation can thus infallibly secure spiritual victory to the Christian soldier, how much more potent he is rendered by the sacramental union with God. Jesus, with divine and human natures, is introduced into the soul. There He is, so to speak, enthroned. Should the passions of the human heart arise in all the violence of a great tempest, and threaten to overwhelm the Christian, will He not rise up and command them to be still? Will His mandate fail to produce a great calm? Ask the fervent and worthily prepared recipient of the holy Communion. He will tell you that Jesus must have addressed some such command to his passions, for after his reception of the Eucharistic Sacrament, a great calm really ensued. The clamoring, noisy voice of passion was entirely hushed. This precious effect of a good Communion ought to satisfy every well-disposed Christian that it is his interest to approach the holy altar *frequently*. Some may ask, What are we to understand by *frequent* Communion? For the benefit of a class of Catholics, unfortunately not a few in numbers, I may say that receiving holy Communion once a year is *not* what is understood by the word *frequent*. Neither can the reception of this Sacrament two or three times in the year be regarded as *frequent* Communion. How often should the faithful approach the holy table? That is to be decided by the confessor for each individual. However, there is no doubt as to the wish of the Church.

Her ardent desire is that her children should lead lives so sinless and holy, as to be worthy to partake of the sacred body and blood as often as they assist at Mass.

IV. The holy Communion is a pledge of eternal life and of a glorious resurrection. This effect is promised by Him whose word shall abide even when heaven and earth shall have passed away: "He that eateth my flesh and drinketh my blood hath everlasting life, and I will raise him up at the last day."

V. The holy Communion is a memorial of the death of our Lord. When Jesus instituted the Eucharistic Sacrifice He intended that the oblation of the Sacrifice and the reception of the Sacrament should serve to remind the people of the mystery of His death. Have you any doubts that such was the Redeemer's intention. Turn to 1 Cor. xi. 26 and you will find that St. Paul removes all doubt: "For as often as you shall eat this bread and drink the chalice, you shew the death of the Lord till he come."

Before concluding this chapter, I have to notice the doctrinal question: Why do the laity receive Communion only under the form of bread? An answer is given not because the children of the Church require it. They have too implicit a confidence in her divine authority, as the Teacher commissioned by Jesus Christ, to question her legislative power in this or any kindred subject. What I shall here say is to enlighten Protestants, at least the honest inquirers among them, and to show Catholics how utterly false and unjust are the charges made against the Church in regard to Communion under one form.

Once more, I feel that I cannot do better than quote the illustrious Bishop

England. He says: "The principal difficulty which our separated brethren make respecting this part of the office is 'the withholding of the cup from the laity,' as they call giving holy Communion only under the appearance of bread. They are under the impression that this is, on our part, a palpable violation of the Divine command, and a gross infraction of the Saviour's institution." . . . . ."There are several facts upon the subject in regard to which we are agreed. During the first eleven centuries it was almost the common practice of the Church to give Communion under both appearances. Next, it is still the general practice of the Greeks and other Orientals, not only of the sects separated from our Church, but also of the portions in our communion, who, however, lawfully follow a peculiar discipline. Again, decrees have been made by the Popes in the fifth century, directing that those who refused to receive under the appearance of wine should be altogether denied Communion; and we also admit that by the Divine institution the person who consecrates the Eucharist, that is, who celebrates Mass, is bound to receive under both kinds as well as to consecrate them. Upon all these points we make the fullest concessions; but neither of these touches the question upon which we differ, viz.: whether it be contrary to the Divine institution, and the nature of the Sacrament, to give Communion in one kind only.

Let us now consider some other facts. Nothing is more clear from Church history than that in private Communion the most usual mode at all times was to receive only under the appearance of bread; sometimes, indeed, under the appearance of wine only; and it was always considered that such Communions were good and sufficient, and by no means contrary to Divine institution. It generally occurred when hermits took the holy Eucharist with them to the places of their retirement; when travelers took it with them to sea or on long journeys into infidel countries; when, during the time of persecution, the faithful were permitted to take it home, that they might have the opportunity of Communion if they should be deprived of their clergy, or if they should themselves be in danger. To these and other similar instances we might add the abstemious, who could not bear the taste or smell of wine, and who were frequently known and admitted amongst the communicants. All these received only under the appearance of bread. The sick generally received under this form only. Children received Communion only under the form of wine. Yet, in every age of the Church, these were considered to have fully partaken of the body and blood of Christ; for His is now a living body, from which the blood is inseparable. Christ rising from the dead, dieth now no more (Romans vi. 9), though, by the words of Consecration, the Lamb is upon the altar, as it were, slain (Apoc. v. 6); the body appears as if separated from the blood; still, when the body is made present, the blood accompanies it of necessity; and when the blood is made present, the body necessarily accompanies it also; so that under either kind, Christ whole and entire, a true Sacrament, is received.

Nor did the Saviour give any precept for those who communicated to receive under both kinds. The expression so frequently quoted to make it appear that He did—viz: "Drink ye all of this" (Matt. xxvi. 27)—was addressed to those to whom He gave the power of consecrating, because they alone were then with Him; and St. Mark informs us that "they all drank of it;" so that the extension of the term used by one Evangelist is precisely defined by the other. It is indeed true that the Saviour did say: "Except you eat the flesh of the Son of man and drink his blood you shall not have life in you" (John vi. 54). But surely the Saviour did not contradict Himself; and He also said (John vi. 52): "If any man eat of this bread, he shall live forever." If He says (verse 55), "He that eateth my flesh and drinketh my blood hath everlasting life," He also informs us (verse 52), "The bread which I will give is my flesh for the life of the world." And though He assures us (verse 57), "He that eateth my flesh and drinketh my blood abideth in me and I in him," yet He promises also (verse 59), "He that eateth this bread shall live forever." The entire difficulty is removed and the passage made consistent, and not contradictory, by the consideration that under either appearance there is really flesh and blood. Hence St. Augustine (Lib. iii. de consens evangel. C. 25) informs us that the Saviour Himself gave Communion under one kind only to the disciples at Emmaus (Luke xxiv. 30, 35), where it is distinctly stated that He vanished after giving them the bread.

St. Paul (1 Cor. xi. 27) states that, "whosoever shall eat this bread, or drink the chalice of the Lord unworthily, shall be guilty of the body and blood of the Lord." It is true that an effort has been made within the last three centuries to change this and many other texts; but from the beginning, the true reading has been given as it is here. The whole text might be easily spared."

The Church finally decreed, that all the ends of the Divine institution are answered by Communion under one species, and that Communion should be administered only under the one species of bread to the laity (Council of Constance, Sess. xiii., confirmed by the bull "In eminentis" of Martin V). This was in the year 1418. The Council of Trent (Sess. xxi. Can. i.) defines: "If any one saith, that by the precept of God, or by necessity of salvation, all and each of the faithful of Christ ought to receive both species of the most holy Sacrament of the Eucharist; let him be anathema." Can. ii.: "If any one saith, that the holy Catholic Church was not induced by just causes and reasons, to communicate, under the species of bread only, laymen, and also clerics when not consecrating; let him be anathema."

The "just causes and reasons" for which the Church has decided that "laymen, and clerics when not consecrating," are to receive Communion under the one species of bread, are chiefly: 1. The danger there always was of the species of wine being spilled, and the holy

Sacrament thereby exposed to profanation. 2. The greater liability of that species becoming sour and corrupting. 3. The difficulty which some persons find in using the species of wine. 4. It was also found that in many places the procuring of a sufficiency of wine for the Sacrifice alone, was not always easy. How much greater embarrassment, were the wine needed for the whole congregation. At all events, from the reasons already assigned, it is manifest that the mode of giving Communion has always been considered in the universal Church a matter of discipline, left by Christ to the regulation of the legislative tribunal, provided always, that it secured, that His body and blood should be given; that this discipline is, and has been, various; that the Latin Church, in the exercise of her right, has ruled, that *for all* except the actually celebrating clergyman, Communion must be under one species, that of bread. Would to God that there were no other difference between us and our Protestant brethren respecting the nature of this most venerable Sacrament.

CHAPTER XXI.

ABLUTIONS—POST-COMMUNION—BLESSING —GOSPEL OF ST. JOHN.

IN the last two chapters some practically useful reflections on the Communion were offered. The attention was to a considerable extent, diverted from strict reflections on the prayers and ceremonies of the Mass. It is, however, hoped that the profit which may be derived from these doctrinal considerations will be more than sufficient to compensate for the interruption.

The priest, after having received the

most precious blood and given holy Communion to the faithful (when there are any communicants), taking the first ablution, says: "Grant, O Lord, that what we have taken with our mouths we may receive with a pure mind, that of a temporal gift it may become to us an eternal remedy." The ablution here spoken of consists of a little wine put into the chalice in order to purify it so that none of the sacred blood may remain therein. He prays during the ablution, and his prayer refers to the holy Communion. He cannot lose sight of that most august and consoling action. Then raising the chalice to his lips, he consumes the wine with which he purified it. Immediately afterward you will notice him taking the sacred cup with both hands and bowing reverently to the Cross upon the tabernacle. After these ceremonies he goes to the Epistle side of the altar, and has wine and water poured upon the fingers which touched the adorable Host. Whilst purifying his fingers he says another prayer, which clearly shows that his whole mind is still filled with the thought of the adorable Sacrament. "May Thy holy body, O Lord, which I have received, and Thy blood which I have drank, cleave to my bowels, and grant that no stain of sin may remain in me who have been fed with this pure and holy Sacrament." The term *bowels* is borrowed from the Sacred Scriptures, and signifies inmost soul (Ps. l. 12; Jeremias xxxi. 33). At the end of this prayer he repairs to the middle of the altar and consumes the second ablution as he did the first. Then, having wiped and dried the chalice, he arranges it as it was before the Offertory. The ceremonies of the ablutions are well calculated to show how minutely exact the Church requires her minister to be in all things pertaining to the respect and reverence due to the most holy Eucharistic Sacrament.

After the purification of the chalice and of his fingers, the priest goes to the Missal, or Mass-book, on the Epistle side, and reads the prayer, termed in the language of the Church the " Communion." This short prayer, which now consists of a verse or two from the Psalms or other parts of the Sacred Scriptures, was formerly an entire psalm sung by the choir during the Communion of the faithful. Hence its present name.

As you perceive, the Church, in the earlier ages of Christianity, even as she now does, availed herself of the powerful aid of music to elevate the hearts of her children to God. At one time, it was the alleluia or hozanna of exultation, awakening sentiments of joy and gladness; at another, it was the plaintive lamentation of a Jeremias, or the penitential strains of the contrite Royal Prophet, fill-ing the hearts of her people with salutary sadness and suffusing the eye with the tears that tell of sorrow and of love. In fine, at other times, it was the funereal chant in which "you imagine that you hear the hollow murmurs of the grave." If a psalm was sung whilst the faithful were receiving the body and blood of Jesus, it was to inspire faith and hope and charity; it was to aid those assisting at the altar, in their efforts to adore with all the fervor of the adoring spirits that environ the throne of the Lamb.

The next prayer is called the Post-Communion. Before saying this prayer, the priest goes to the middle of the altar and kisses it, and, having turned to the people, salutes them, saying: "Dominus vobiscum"—"The Lord be with you." This salutation, which we have heard so often during the Sacrifice, is a most appropriate wish after the holy Communion. Having returned to the Book and made the usual reverence to the Cross, he invites the faithful to unite with him in the Post-Communion, or prayer, in which he returns thanks to God for the holy Sacrifice and Sacrament, and implores the grace necessary to profit by them. Whilst making mention of the thanksgiving here made by the priest in the Mass, it is proper to remind the faithful that they too, after having received the holy Sacrament, should, if possible, spend at least fifteen minutes in returning thanks for this ineffable blessing. The practice of leaving the church *as soon as* Mass is finished, is much to be deplored.

On some occasions the Post-Communion consists of several prayers. At the end of these fervent expressions of gratitude and supplication, you see the priest going again to the middle of the altar, and kissing it. Then rising and turning towards the people, he again salutes them, and immediately adds: "Ite missa est"—"Go, you are dismissed." Here the prayers of Mass ended ordinarily. On some particular occasions, in which the faithful continued in prayer for some time after the termination of the holy Sacrifice, instead of "Ite missa est," the priest, turning to the altar, invited the flock to continue in prayer: "Benedicamus Domino"—"Let us bless the Lord."

Though the Mass, strictly speaking, is finished at the words "Ite missa est," still, at the request of the faithful, the priest's blessing and some verses of the first chapter of the Gospel according to St. John were added. To impart his blessing, the priest, turning to the altar and bowing down in the attitude of reverence, says the following prayer: "Let the performance of my homage be pleasing to Thee, O holy Trinity; and grant that the Sacrifice which I, though unworthy, have offered up in the sight of Thy Majesty, may be acceptable to Thee, and through Thy mercy be a propitiation for me and all those for whom it has been offered. Through Christ our Lord. Amen." Then, rising, he invokes the blessing of the Omnipotent God upon the faithful, and, turning to the congregation, as the vicegerent of the Most High, he imparts that benediction in the name of the Father, Son, and Holy Ghost. The people desired the priest's blessing, knowing full well that "to bless" is one of the privileges of the priest of the Gospel Dispensation—one of the special powers conferred upon him in his ordination.

Special devotion to the Gospel of St. John led to the introduction of the first verses of it into the Mass. Indeed it is a solemn and admirably opportune profession of our faith in the great mystery of the Incarnation—the fountain-head of all the other mysteries consummated in time through the mercy of God in behalf of mankind. Those fourteen verses of the admirable Gospel of St. John are: "In the beginning was the Word, and the Word was with God, and the Word was God. The same was in the beginning with God. All things were made by him: and without him was made nothing that was made. In him was life, and the life was the light of men: and the light shineth in darkness, and the darkness did not comprehend it. There was a man sent from God, whose name was John. This man came for a witness, to bear witness of the light, that all men might believe through him. He was not the light, but was to give testimony of the light. That was the true light which enlighteneth every man that cometh into this world. He was in the world, and the world was made by him; and the world knew him not. He came unto his own, and his own received him not.

But as many as received him, he gave them power to be made the sons of God, to them that believe in his name: who are born, not of blood, nor of the will of the flesh, nor of the will of man. And the Word was made flesh, and dwelt among us (and we saw his glory, the glory, as it were, of the only-begotten of the Father), full of grace and truth (St. John i. 1-14). To these divinely inspired words, to this sublime account of the mystery of the Incarnation, the assembled faithful, by their representative, the clerk, respond in heartfelt gratitude, "Deo gratias"—"Thanks be to God." At these words the priest returns to the middle of the altar, bows to the Cross, goes down to the foot of the altar, bends the knee once more in adoration, and retires to the sacristy, where he unvests.

It is only at this moment, when the officiating minister has retired, that the faithful should begin to go out of the church. Indeed they would do well to remain a few moments to utter words of thanks for the great mysteries at which they have assisted. This would be to enter into the spirit of the last words of the sacred liturgy: " Deo gratias "— "Thanks be to God."

CONCLUSION.

Y purpose in penning these pages was sufficiently stated in the Introduction. However, I once more beg leave to remind my readers that I have written for such as, for one reason or another, have had very little opportunity to obtain instruction on the important subject treated in this volume. Moral reflections predominate, because my chief purpose has been to move the Catholic heart to the most fervent devotion toward the adorable Sacrament and Sacrifice of the Altar. Liturgical explanations of the principal ceremonies prescribed for the

oblation of the great Christian Sacrifice were deemed equally important, and perhaps no less conducive to the securing of earnest piety in those assisting at the holy Mass. The grandeurs and salutary significance of our incomparable ceremonial have been unveiled, it is hoped, to the advantage of both Catholic and Protestant readers. The doctrinal considerations, found here and there, were designed: (1) to point out to Catholics the teachings of that Church which they revere and love; (2) to show the faithful how groundless, futile and unjust are the objections made by our separated brethren against one or other article of our faith or ceremonial observance; (3) to enable Protestants to see the Catholic faith and ceremonial as they are in reality, in order that they may learn to distrust the misrepresentations which ignorance or malice has made.

Will my humble efforts be productive

of the good results which I most ardently desire? I am, of course, unable to say. However, if they conduce to make one Catholic more fervent at the foot of the altar during the adorable Sacrifice, one Protestant more earnest in search of God's holy truth, my labor will have been repaid.

Love for the hidden God of our altar prompted me to write. Love now prompts me to place what I have written as an offering of love at the feet of that same hidden God abiding in the Eucharistic Tabernacle. May He bless it and render it conducive to the spiritual interests of those whom He loves so well.

THE END.

www.ingramcontent.com/pod-product-compliance
Lightning Source LLC
Chambersburg PA
CBHW021157230426
43667CB00006B/435